VALUE
ACCELERATION

VALUE
ACCELERATION

the secrets to building an
unbeatable competitive advantage

MITCHELL GOOZÉ
& RALPH MROZ

Published by Elevate, Charleston, South Carolina.
Member of Advantage Media Group.

ELEVATE is a registered trademark and the
Elevate colophon is a trademark of Advantage Media Group, Inc.

Printed in the United States of America

ISBN: 978-1-60194-004-9

Most Advantage Media Group titles are available at special quantity discounts for bulk purchases for sales promotions, premiums, fundraising, and educational use. Special versions or book excerpts can also be created to fit specific needs.

For more information, please write: Special Markets, Advantage Media Group, P.O. Box 272, Charleston, SC 29402 or call 1.866.775.1696.

Dedications

From Mitch:

To my wife Carol, who has put up with and supported my work in this area for most of our life together.

From Ralph:

To Barbara, who both as my former boss and my wife, not only encouraged me to pursue this work, but contributed to it.

Contents

Acknowledgements

This work is the result of several years of collective effort by us and our colleagues at Customer Manufacturing Group. Without the support and contributions of Bayard Bookman, Jeff Krawitz and Neil Reckon, the entire package would have never come together.

We also acknowledge the contributions of Robert Johnson, Tom Saichek, and Jim Shaw in reviewing early drafts of the manuscript. Special thanks go to Joan Pastor for her suggestion (insistence) for the inclusion of the fable and to Jeff Davidson for his help in writing it.

Thanks also to Peter LaPlaca who, as Editor of *Industrial Marketing Management*, published the work of an unknown, which was the catalyst for bringing us together.

FOREWORD

Value creation, both from a societal and a micro-economic viewpoint, is the result of meeting the demands of your customers. Understanding those demands and aligning them with the capabilities of your enterprise is the process by which you most fundamentally create value. Everything else you do is in support of this most basic process. Excelling at this process is, in the end, your only real strategic advantage.

This book focuses on accelerating your value creation efforts. Not only by making them faster, but by helping you get it right the first time ... because you may not get a next time.

PROLOGUE — A FABLE

THE SECRET PROCESS AND THE SEARCH FOR COMPETITIVE ADVANTAGE

At Great West Industries, the last quarter had been the worst yet. Sales were down 5% while competitor FastGear's were up 11%. One of the casualties of this continuing decline was Marketing Director Jerry Rodgers who had been laid off. The logical place for him to look for a job was at FastGear. With his resume and management experience, Jerry landed a job interview with Jason Beckley, FastGear's president.

"Good morning, Jerry. I understand you want to join our marketing department. Tell me about your experience at Great West."

"Well, after getting beat up on costs and lead times for a few years, we finally invested in a thoroughly modern manufacturing process. We revamped our production schedules, instituted a JIT and a six-sigma program, and got our ERP software up and running, finally. We had a cracker-jack sales force — we'd hired only the best in the industry — and our finance and HR departments had won industry awards for progressive practices. We did a lot of things right! We may not have been the first kids on the block to institute new practices, but when we did, we did them well."

"Did it help?" Jason asked.

"Sure. Last quarter we only lost 1.7 percent of our market share. Mostly to you guys!"

"How do you figure that happened?" Jason asked, smiling.

"Well, you guys are about 50 years old — as old as Great West. Until seven years ago, we were both pretty competitive with each other, although Great West always had the larger market share in the areas where our products overlapped. About seven years ago, though, you started getting into the new, fast-growing market areas ahead of us, and now you have more market share than they do. You're growing faster, too."

They talked more and Jason admitted that, unquestionably, Jerry could be a good catch for FastGear, but at the moment there wasn't an open position at his level.

"You've come at a reasonably good time," Jason said. "We're glad you applied and; if things work out, we hope you're willing to 'sub-optimize' for a quarter, until we can get you into the right slot."

Jason continued, "I think once you're fully immersed in our processes you could be a great asset. I'd like you to talk to some of our people," Jason said, "Let's see who's available today."

While waiting, Jerry read some FastGear literature that he'd been given. His reading reacquainted him with many of the facts that he'd forgotten over the last several years. He was captivated by the fact that FastGear hadn't failed to capitalize on a single important market opportunity during the previous seven-plus years. In terms of market share and customer count, they were growing at twice the rate of everyone else in the industry. He thought to himself, *What in the world are they doing?*

THE INTERVIEW WITH DESIGN ENGINEERING

Jason returned and walked Jerry into an office near his. A woman was there to greet him. "Hi, I'm Amy Wyndom," she said. "I'm a design manager for one of our product lines. Jason asked me to show you around."

Amy gave Jerry the quick tour and introduced him to some of the staff, leaving Jerry with Steve Ellison, and went back to her office. Steve showed Jerry one of his current projects. "Check these out!" he said. "New ideas for product upgrades."

"Where did all those ideas come from?" Jerry asked.

"Marketing — actually product management and market research."

"How does marketing generate design ideas?"

"Who else?" asked Steve with surprise.

Jerry's stomach tightened a bit. He realized that, in theory, marketing should be in the lead, new product-wise, but ... well, it had just never worked that way at Great West. The engineers at Great West had always seemed to drive the new products that were made and marketing had taken a back seat or support role — not that the results were all that great, of course.

"How could marketing not come up with ideas?" Steve continued. "After all, they are the ones who are constantly watching the market."

"Sure," Jerry interrupted, "Marketing tracks market share information and does competitive analyses." Actually, *that's what we wished they would do,* Jerry was thinking. *All they really did, though, at Great West, was advertising and promotion.*

"No," Steve interjected, "That's only a small piece of what they do. Sure, marketing here tracks industry data every which way you can imagine. And they do product competitive analyses, too. But they also do deep customer needs and usage analyses. Heck, we know more about our customers in terms of our product usage than any of our customers themselves — or channel partners — probably know. Marketing also does competitive analyses in terms of absolutely everything relevant about the competition — their finances, manufacturing, product development, management ... you name it. They track the societal factors and government regulations that affect us. They know the business model, sales compensation schemes, and a reasonable estimate of the item-by-item costs and prof-itability of the competition — including Great West. I'm kinda scratching the surface ... but product feature tables and market segment growth rates are only a tiny piece of what marketing does here. Not to overstep, but, is this new to you?"

Jerry finessed his way around the pointed question and then asked, "You mentioned product management?"

"'Product management' is our term for the marketing people that work with the engineers throughout the new product development cycle," Steve said. "About ten years ago we, like so many others in the industry, instituted a phase-review product development process. It worked great — we cut cycle time in half and we hit a few more market windows. But everyone else in the industry had done the same thing, so we were really just staying at par in terms of competitive position and market growth."

Jerry's stomach tightened again. *Great West had only put a structured product development process in place three years ago,* he thought.

Steve went on: "What was happening was, the old garbage-in/garbage-out game. We had a very effective new product development process, but we didn't have an equally effective marketing process that linked to it — to tell our engineers what to make and when, and work with them throughout the process at greater and greater levels of detail. Now we do, as part of our overall marketing process, and things are much better."

Jerry's stomach was not getting any more relaxed. *Great West's engineers and mar-*

keting people barely talked to each other, he thought. After a bit more conversation, the meeting with Steve wrapped up and Jerry went on to meet with several other key managers throughout the division before heading back to Amy's office.

THE INTERVIEW WITH AMY

Jerry was mulling over the fact that the product development function at FastGear was so tightly integrated with market research through the product management function and he mentioned this to Amy. "Our product managers at Great West focused on promotion and field support," he said, "You seem to have a different approach."

"Actually," Amy said, "We have those people too, only we call their activity product marketing. They are focused on the product after it's been introduced, while our product managers are focused on the development phase of the product. We find that they really are two distinct jobs, and require different sets of skills and backgrounds."

Jerry had a ton more questions. "I can see that you've tightly coupled your product development process with marketing, but where's the strategic element? How do you decide what your overall marketing strategy and positioning is? How do you tie together your various product development efforts into a strategic whole? Let alone, how do you do resource allocation?" Jerry asked these questions partly because he wanted to know FastGear's answer and partly because these had been such sticking points at Great West.

Amy wasn't hesitant at all. "I think Steve described the spectrum of data that our market research department generates, yes?"

Jerry nodded.

"Actually," she continued, "Our entire marketing department generates this ongoing data, but market research spearheads the continuous collection and analysis of it. Well, once you know virtually everything about your market, your customers, the products in your space, the competition and everything about the other things that influence your business, making strategic decisions isn't all that hard. This information comes together in a way that forms patterns that experienced people can see. Actually, identifying the opportunities in the market and throwing them against available resources and corporate strategy is a pretty straightforward activity — not easy, mind you, not easy at all — but reasonably straightforward."

Jerry felt his stomach tightening again. *This wasn't remotely straightforward at Great West,* he thought. In fact, trying to figure out strategic direction was a hugely frustrating exercise there. *We wasted so much time arguing over who was right, that it was a miracle that anything ever got done,* he thought to himself. *Come to think of it, very little had gotten done lately.*

Instead of voicing these thoughts though, Jerry asked, "So you have a standard process for making these decisions?" He hoped that he'd get a silver bullet of insight here.

"Oh yes," said Amy, "We have periodic management meetings devoted to setting strategic direction, allocating resources, and reviewing our current direction. These were black holes of wasted time before we got our act together, but now that we have reasonably complete data to make these decisions on, and feedback about our ongoing activities, these meetings are actually fun. Now we can argue over the important things," she laughed.

"So it's the data that's your secret," Jerry said.

"No, it's the *process,*" said Amy, "The data is a result of the process; the decisions are a result of the process, the products are a result of the process, the promotion is a result of the process … the *process* is everything."

Promotion, thought Jerry: advertising, lead generation, trade shows, public relations. That's what marketing most meant to him. *What about that?,* he wondered.

"What do you folks do about promotion?" he asked.

"Let me introduce you to Ben," she said.

THE INTERVIEW WITH MARKETING COMMUNICATIONS

Amy took Jerry up to the next floor, where she introduced him to Ben Martin, the Marketing Communications manager for the product line. His office had the creative look of someone with that function.

After a few moments of conversation, Jerry asked, "I've been introduced to your marketing process, in terms of market research, product development and strategy, but what you do is what I really think of when I say the word 'marketing.'

How does your function fit in?"

"Ah-hah," said Ben, "That's a common mistake. Most people think 'promotion' when they hear 'marketing.' Actually, I used to, too. But then when I came here a few years ago, I saw the bigger picture. What you've seen with Steve and Amy is what we call the 'front end' of marketing. That is, the things that have to logically be done first. First, you have to have data — about the market, the customers, the competition, etc., right? Then you have to use that data to set a direction in terms of positioning and product strategy. ... Still with me? Then you can focus on lower levels of strategy — promotional strategy, sales strategy, customer relationship strategy, etc. Yes? Then, and only then, can you intelligently embark on actually doing promotion, which is what I mostly manage. We call that the 'back end' of marketing. My function eats a lot of money, as you can imagine, and we are pretty concerned that we have our activities aligned to support strategies and products — otherwise, we can wind up throwing away a lot of cash."

Don't I know it, thought Jerry. "How do you get that alignment?" he asked.

"The *process*," said Ben. "The *process*."

A SAMPLE OF THE PROCESS

Jerry thought that his meetings were nearly over when Amy greeted him in the hallway and said she wanted to show him one more thing. He followed her down the hall and she had him sit down at the large table. "Jason thought it might be worthwhile if you participated in some of our decision-making, so that you could get a hands on idea of what you'd be doing here," she said.

"Here is the data," she said. "We need to decide on a total of four new products that fit the market demand — both current and future. These are not brand-new, big products — those would be decided at a series of strategy meetings. Rather, these are smaller products or product variations, the need for which seems apparent from our ongoing market research and field activities."

"Field activities...?" said Jerry, "You mean sales?"

"Sales and field support — technical support, customer support, etc," said Amy.

That stomach thing again. *Great West could never even get sales and marketing to have civil conversations*, he thought.

Jerry was amazed by the depth, clarity, and timeliness of the market data staring him in the face. Standard market research data from public sources, analyses of that data, and data from industry organizations were included, as were data from internal sources and analyses of data from the sales force and the various field organizations. Jerry studied the research and the designs. He ultimately chose three designs that best met the customer needs. He found a fourth that had potential but was missing the type of rechargeable battery that customers appeared to want. Amy concurred with his selections.

For the first time in who knows how long, Jerry felt like he'd made an informed decision — all in the space of ... what? ... twenty minutes?

Jerry reflected on how these decisions would have been made at Great West. They put off decisions like these sometimes for months, after which the data — he now realized — was sufficiently old as to be irrelevant. Times had changed since Great West Industries' heyday. By the time they got around to meeting a demand, the demand had changed. Why did they always lag behind demand? There was no process for capitalizing on — or even recognizing — market changes when they began.

BACK TO THE CEO

Afterwards, Jerry went to speak with Jason as the end to the day's activities. During this second visit with Jason, Jerry was determined to find out just what this process was that everyone had talked about.

Jerry arrived in the office, and, as before, Jason invited him to sit. "What more can I tell you about FastGear?" Jason asked.

"What's behind it? What's the secret?" Jerry blurted out, "You're growing faster than anyone in the industry, you haven't missed a major opportunity in over five years, and from what I've seen here today, you've licked a number of internal problems that hold everyone else back."

Jason laughed. "Well, it's certainly no secret. We've had enough articles written about us in the business press. First, we have a process for everything that's critical to profitability, and the processes are interconnected. We recognized early on that you can't have a process for production only; the 'assembly line' era has long passed. You also can't just have a process for design. I mean, who cares how fast you can design and produce goods if they're not the right goods? Our 'secret,' if that's what it is, is that we have now instituted a structured process for marketing — all of marketing, not just promotion. As you saw today, we have a marketing process that incorporates and integrates research, strategy, product development, promotion and sales. This marketing process is linked and integrated with every other corporate process. So now the entire company is process driven … with no holes in or gaps between the processes."

"I've never heard of a marketing process like this before," said Jerry

"It's the next challenge in management," said Jason. "Every other function in the company has been 'processized' by now — at least by any competitive company. So where does competitive advantage come from now — now that you can buy a good process for almost any other function 'out of the box', so to speak?"

Answering his own question, Jason continued, "It comes from doing all of that well — having a world-class process in operations and so on — meeting the ante of the industry, if you will — and then going the next step. Which in this case is to add a true marketing process. That's been the missing element until now. It hasn't existed until recently."

"So it's risky," said Jerry.

"No," said Jason. "What is risky is not initiating valid management techniques before the competition does."

"How's that not risky? The conventional wisdom is to wait and see how other companies do before you spend the resources to jump into something new," responded Jerry.

"Yes, but competitive advantage will go to those companies that have successful implementations of new techniques first. That's obvious, right?"

Uh-duh, thought Jerry.

"Well, that means that you have to be the first to get going on them. If you wait until something is tried and true, then all you are ever doing is playing catch-up. That's a losing game."

That struck a nerve with Jerry. Great West had for many years been one of the last in their industry to implement new methods. It was only their competition taking business away from them with those new methods that caused Great West to act at all.

"But there's risk in new management methods," said Jerry, a bit defensive about the role he himself had sometimes played at Great West in "going slow" with regard to new ideas.

"There's risk in not adopting them, too," said Jason. "Think of it this way: while the leaders are refining their implementations of new methods, the followers are just embarking on their own initial implementation. Which is the better position to be in?"

Jerry couldn't argue with that logic. "So that's the secret," he said, "What I can't figure out is why you're telling me — heck, you're telling the whole world — about it. Don't you want to literally keep it a 'secret'?"

"No point," said Jason. "You see, every company is already predisposed — by their management and by their culture — to embrace change or not. Those that actually seek out change will always be the first to adopt new methods, while those that resist it will never use them until its too late. The first kind of company is our real competition and there's nothing we can do to stop them from learning about how we operate. The other kind of company wouldn't do anything with the knowledge even if we FedEx'ed it to them, so they are no threat whatsoever. From our perspective, they are a self-correcting problem, if you follow me."

Jerry did indeed. He thought about the image of Great West's CEO finding FastGear's "secret" process on his desk one morning. Jason was right. Nothing would've happened!

"We haven't talked about sales," said Jerry, "How do you specify your sales process? How do you make it efficient?"

"We don't design our sales process!" declared Jason. "And efficiency isn't our primary concern anyway!"

Jerry felt like he'd just been bushwhacked. "Huh?" he asked. "Don't you link your sales process to your marketing process — and everything else, too?"

"Of course we do," said Jason

"But," interrupted Jerry, "You just said you don't design your sales process…"

"Right," interjected a smiling Jason, "But there are a couple key points you haven't discussed with our people yet. Hopefully, we'll cover that ground later. We'd like to have you come back next week for a next round of interviews. Does that work for you?"

Jerry nodded his agreement...

INTRODUCTION

The situations are all too familiar:

- An established company, no longer a young start-up, is beginning to falter. Growth isn't what it was, profit margins are falling and customers aren't lining up at the door anymore. The original management team is finally trying some new marketing approaches—a new approach every quarter, it seems—and none are very successful.

- The new technology start-up, staffed with experienced people from established companies, has a hot new product. Management has a healthy respect for the power of marketing, but has trouble articulating just what "marketing" is, and the new company's marketing efforts are sluggish in getting off the ground. In any case, the focus always seems to be on the product and technology issues.

- The company is introducing a new product, or starting a new product line, or targeting a new market. A marketing plan is needed and an awful lot of management's time is devoted to figuring out what "marketing" will be *this time*.

- New products or services too often don't meet expectations. This could be caused by ineffective product launches, the wrong product, the wrong target market, or maybe… There's plenty of blame, but the problem continues.

- The mature firm — comfortably profitable for so long — is seeing margins erode and customers lost to more nimble competitors, in the face of rapid market change. The firm understands that it has been a bit lax in its past marketing efforts and wants to rectify the situation. But where to begin? And what is "marketing" anyway?

As we progress through the information economy, it has become clear that the strength of a corporation's processes[1] determines whether the company can anticipate its future markets and adapt to them ... or be surprised by them — perhaps

---

1. The Random House dictionary defines a "process" as a systematic series of actions directed to some end. This is clearly applicable to the desired result of marketing/sales. Marketing/Sales can clearly be viewed as a process. The fact that the desired result is often not achieved, or at least not consistently achieved, is usually due to the lack of appropriate management.

fatally. In this age, characterized by frenetic and unpredictable change, the marketplace alone no longer provides a stable reference to guide and correct corporate activities. Therefore, the corporation's processes themselves must be stable and coherent in order for the company to remain in sync with the market.

With the acceptance in the 1990s of the necessity of a stable, structured, and repeatable product development process, only the marketing function was left without an overall integrating process model — which not only integrates the multitude of activities that constitute marketing, *but also* integrates marketing seamlessly with other business functions, such as sales and product development. The lack of a useful model and a method for managing the marketing and the integrated marketing/sales[2] function is at the root of most of the ongoing problems commonly seen in "marketing."

This book argues the case for the necessity of such a structured, unified marketing/sales model and for objective methods to manage it. It then presents an overview of the first instance of a useful integrated marketing/sales model[3] and demonstrates how universal management methods that have been applied successfully to manufacturing apply equally well to marketing/sales.

The economy of the major industrial nations is now entering its fourth stage. We have passed through the agrarian and industrial economies, based on the critical resources of labor and capital respectively. Today, most industries are exiting the post-industrial economic stage. This stage was based on the critical resource of traditional management skills. We have entered what some are calling the "information economy" stage based on the critical resource of process management skills. Many people have pointed out that, in this new age, competitive advantage comes to those enterprises with the most effective processes. That is, a process-centric management focus and organization replaces a task-centric perspective and management style.

2. In this book, we will argue that marketing and sales are two poles of one overall corporate process. It is for this reason that we refer to that overall process as marketing/sales. At the same time, we recognize that marketing and sales are two separate elements in this process, albeit with a fair amount of overlap. When we are referring to the overall process, we will use the term marketing/sales. When we wish to differentiate the two elements—and they are often confused—we will use the individual words marketing and sales.

3. It is critical to note the important difference between a market model and a marketing/sales model. Companies have for many years attempted, with varying degrees of success, to model markets and to use those models to determine actions to improve the likelihood of success with products/services designed to serve those markets. This is inherently different from a marketing/sales model that is created to facilitate the ability to manage the process of marketing/sales within a company, regardless of the markets it is attempting to serve or the market models it may choose to use to assist in that work.

This change requires a clear understanding of the processes that form the foundation of the enterprise. The process-centric corporation is made up of many interlocking processes — some functional and some *cross-functional*. Indeed, the success of cross-functional corporate processes will stand on the foundation of strong functional skills and processes.

This last point is still not well understood. With all of the (deserved) attention that "customer-centric" processes — which are almost always, necessarily cross-functional — have received in the past decade, it's all too easy to forget that *functional skills are the basis of these customer-centric, cross-functional processes.* (Actually, "multi-functional" might be a more accurate term than "cross-functional.")

Product Development is an example of a cross-functional corporate process that is largely composed of functional engineering skills and is dependent upon functional engineering — or product development (in the usual sense of the term) — processes. Likewise, Product Development (as a cross-functional process) includes many functional marketing activities. To be successful, it must be closely coupled with a coherent, integrated, functional marketing process. With the lack of such an integrating marketing process, many so-called cross functional Product Development processes now in formation are simply excellent traditional product development processes — which is no small feat, but which still fall short of the mark.

As Peter Drucker has pointed out, marketing, properly understood and practiced, is the very soul of the enterprise — it gives meaning to and permeates all aspects of it: "*...the business enterprise has two — and only these two — basic functions: marketing and innovation ... all the rest are "costs."*" It has taken decades to realize the truth of this prescient statement, but it is now becoming startlingly clear. If a clear understanding and rigorous management of the enterprise's processes is critical to its success, then a clear understanding and rigorous management of the enterprise's marketing/sales process is foundational. The processes previously developed and implemented by corporations have largely been to make the company more efficient. Process management of the marketing/sales process will also make the company more effective.[5]

And yet, today, few people can confidently define marketing or sales, let alone

---

4. Peter F. Drucker, People and Performance (New York: Harper College Press, 1977), 90.

5. To ensure clarity, efficiency is doing things right. Effectiveness is doing the right thing.

apply them as part of an integrated process of hierarchical activities that fuse with other corporate processes. At the very root of these problems is the lack of an overarching, unified *model* of marketing/sales.

Your company already creates value — or it wouldn't be in business. But merely creating value is yesterday's game. The locus of competition is now moving to *accelerating* the rate of value creation, or to **value acceleration**. This book provides the key to value acceleration — the *process-based* key to hitting the right market at the right time with the right product in the right way — the first time, because you may not get a second time. Process management has always been at the foundation of everything sustainable that an enterprise accomplished. Now it is seeing a renewed focus and respect. *Value Acceleration* takes process management to its last frontier, to the core of your only sustainable competitive advantage.

IS YOUR COMPANY EQUIPPED FOR VALUE ACCELERATION?

1

C H A P T E R   O N E

the foundation of
value acceleration

In the information economy of the 21st Century, corporate survival depends on the effectiveness of the corporation's innate business processes. In fact, many corporations will be defined not so much by their industry or products, but by the nature of their processes — particularly processes that promote innovation. Survival depends on superior accuracy in identifying new opportunities; the ability to match those opportunities with corporate capabilities so as to develop products/services in a timely way; and the ability to promote and sell those products/services effectively.

Today, the pace of change in capital, skill requirements, and technology is not merely rapid, but outright frenetic. It is impossible to compare it to the economy of the 1980s, or even your father's economy, much less any that have gone before.

The so-called "first world economy" is now entering its fourth stage. The agrarian economy lasted roughly from pre-history until the turn of the 20th Century. The industrial economy, based on manufacturing and sales capability, lasted until roughly the mid-1980s. The post-industrial economy, which is now coming to an end, will last for a short time in the 21st Century. During the late industrial period (between 1950-1985), sales and promotion supplanted manufacturing as the primary competitive arena. Starting in the mid-1980s, the product development function became the battleground, as the post-industrial stage began.

Industrial and even post-industrial economies were relatively stable. Their capital movement, their labor-skills requirements, and, most importantly, their rate of technological change, were all fairly easy to understand, follow, and, to an enviable degree, predict. These factors, in general, changed dramatically over the course of one generation. Managers of institutions in previous economies not only had the time, but the ability to respond to these changes. Not so today.

This is the era of the synchronous organization. Opportunity identification, capabilities matching, product development, production, promotion and sales must all be synchronized or the company, unable to adapt to its environment, will die. This necessitates real-time information flows and real-time decision making.[6] The metaphor is not so much a road race, where the end point and path to it are known in advance, but an orienteering race, where only the general direction is known ahead of time and navigation is done on the fly. In fact, success is largely determined by the ability to make correct navigational decisions in real time.

To paraphrase Peter Drucker's well-known jazz analogy: The previous management model was that of an orchestra, with the conductor (CEO) coordinating the players, all of whom had the same score. By contrast, "what we are talking about today are diversified groups [like a jazz ensemble] that have to write the score while they perform."[7]

A company's marketing process — and its integration with other business functions, including its sales process and product-development process — is the remaining functional battleground in this war for corporate survival.

ADDITIVE ABILITIES

The number of corporate abilities necessary to function at any given time is always increasing. In the early industrial economy, manufacturing competence was what mattered most. Then distribution abilities became important. Later, the ability to promote effectively (for the times) was added to the burden of abilities necessary for corporate survival. Ultimately, the ability to develop products in an efficient and effective way became crucial, as well.

---

6. Business 2.0 reported in its March 2003 issue about a recent initiative by GE Plastics to cre-ate a digital cockpit to allow managers to answer the question, "How's this quarter looking?" in real time with a consistent answer, rather than the then-existing response, which depended on whom you asked.

7. Wired, August 1996, p. 119

Even today, it is apparent that the skills and abilities an enterprise must have to survive are additive — that is, new skills are constantly required in addition to previously required skills. Another way of saying this is, that the "skills price" or "competency hurdle" of doing business is constantly increasing. As a simple example: when telephones were first invented, they represented a source of competitive advantage (and expense) to those firms that had them. But when everyone had them, their ability to provide competitive advantage disappeared, though the necessity of having them did not. Telephones became part of the entry fee, the ante, or the "baseline cost of doing business." In fact, once numerous competitors master any corporate competency, the bar is raised. That competency becomes the new baseline cost of doing business. And the battle for customers and profits moves on to the next front.

That more and more competencies are required just to stay in business is not surprising, since experience, as well as common sense, tells us that the cost of acquiring new skills is dear, while the cost of maintaining previously acquired skills is cheap. This is true whether we are talking about individuals or organizations. Learning a new language is difficult, but maintaining fluency in one is easy. Achieving aerobic fitness is painful, but maintaining it is fun. Building an effective manufacturing, sales, or product development process is both painful and difficult, but retaining one is much less so.

By the same token, organizational skills, like individual skills, require energy to maintain. Language fluency and aerobic capacity can be lost without regular practice. And, although there are numerous examples of companies that have maintained a high level of organizational skills for decades, management incompetence can allow those skills to dissipate. Even an excellent product development process — like any other process — can wither away without rigorous management.

It should be obvious that achievements in competence are not end-goals, but rather steps on a continuous ladder. However, this point is seldom grasped. "In a survey taken at the end of the 1980s, nearly 80% of U.S. managers believed that quality (an industrial-stage skill) would be a fundamental source of competitive advantage in the year 2000 (as we entered the information age)."[8] Yet it is important to note that quality disappeared as a source of competitive advantage long before 2000 — it simply became a baseline cost of doing business.

8. Frank V. Cespedes, Concurrent Marketing, (Cambridge: Harvard Business School Press, 1995), p. 126

THE BASIS OF COMPETITIVE ADVANTAGE: CRITICAL AND POST-CRITICAL-STAGE SKILLS

Throughout most of the industrial and post-industrial age, the basis of competitive advantage has been a corporation's functional competence, usually with one functional ability — *the critical functional skill* — dominating. From the turn of the century to about 1950, those companies who could manufacture more efficiently and effectively than their competitors won the market—low product cost was the critical functional skill and the ticket to profitability. Of course, other corporate functions — such as, sales, finance, development, and so on—had to be comparatively strong too, because a serious weakness in any one of them could cripple a company. But, as a rule, while weaknesses in other functions could hurt the company, the function that conveyed competitive advantage — *the critical functional skill* — was manufacturing.

Likewise, from 1950 to 1985 or so, the dominant functional basis of competitive advantage was traditional sales and promotion.[9] Naturally, manufacturing, as a baseline skill for competitive advantage, continued to be a necessity — in fact, this function entered its *post-critical-stage phase*. During this time of stable, low-cost manufacturing — with the ascendancy of sales and promotional effectiveness as the competitive differentiator — the focus on the manufacturing function migrated to its post-critical-stage locus: high quality. This is the natural state of affairs. Functional skills do not ever vanish as a necessity for competitive advantage.

After a functional competence has been accomplished, the dominant competitive arena simply moves onto another functional area — or to another defining corporate characteristic altogether — while the previous critical functional area continues to be a competitive locus throughout the development of secondary or post-critical-stage skills.

---

9. The delineation of industrial stages presented in this chapter diverges here from the traditional, industrial-stage view; which, as a general rule, asserts that traditional sales were predominant, from about 1950 to 1970, after which, we entered the marketing stage, which some believe we are now exiting. This divergence in views goes to the heart of the thesis of this book. We believe that marketing as generally practiced and operationally defined by the traditional, industrial-stage view was really not much more than the back-end of marketing; in other words, mostly promotional activities (i.e., sales support), not an integrated, unified practice of the complete responsibilities of the marketing function.

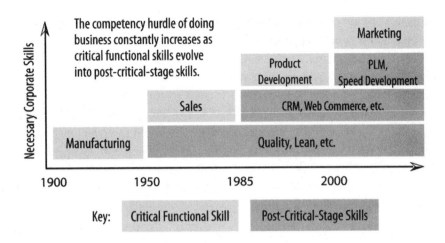

Figure 1-1

Product development began to take over as the competitively differentiating or critical functional skill in the mid-1980s. Here the competitive differentiators were time-to-market and high quality in complex products/services. Of course, manufacturing continued to become more and more efficient through the use of post-critical-stage skills, such as lean inventory management, manufacturing automation, computerization, and a design-for-manufacture-based tie-in to product development. The effectiveness of traditional sales and promotion continued to be refined too, through post-critical-stage skills, such as web commerce, CRM, sales-force automation, database marketing, and so on.[10]

MARKETING/SALES TO BE THE CRITICAL FUNCTIONAL SKILL

In the 21st Century, the integration of marketing with product development and sales to form a true and integrated marketing/sales process (that links to product development) is the critical functional skill. For example, many of the problems that corporations — even those with world-class product development organizations — see today can be traced to the "garbage-in/garbage-out" phenomena. When marketing cannot tell product development what to make when, when it is not capable of being a full, integrated partner throughout the development cycle, then the effectiveness of the product development process is blunted.[11]

---

10. Note that the time frames given in this section are generalizations — rough averages for the U.S. economy as a whole. Naturally, any specific U.S. industry goes through these stages on its own unique time table, as do non-U.S. economies.

11. This important linkage between marketing and product development is discussed in more detail in Chapter 12.

In this marketing-dominated era, when effective product development (engineering) processes are assumed, the critical skills become: features/benefits/value articulation and prediction; market timing; positioning management; and management of the customer-adaptation cycle.

As was pointed out in *The Secret to Selling More*,[12] marketing's role in increasing sales is also critical. Beyond the importance of integrating marketing with sales, to form one overall marketing/sales process, is the need for more effective tools with which to manage this process. An integrated-process model and objective management methods to manage that process lay the foundation for realizing the potential of marketing/sales.

With respect to marketing, per se: the "back-end" marketing skills of promotion and sales support are currently reasonably well understood and refined, and they can be implemented well by any organization with the desire to do so. However, the "front-end" marketing skills — such as positioning and opportunity identification — and the "integrative" marketing skills — such as integration with product development, sales and corporate strategy—are not well understood. It is in this holistic sense that a truly useful marketing/sales process model addresses the marketing function.

CORE COMPETENCIES

The concept of *core competencies*, introduced by Prahalad and Hamel in 1990,[13] casts the notion of critical functional skills in a post-industrial light. Their thesis is that many successful companies build product lines and market presences around core competencies, which are usually a technical or a manufacturing skill that permeates the organization. The twist is their conclusion that, when these functional skills are dominant across product and market spaces, true synergy results.

The practice of developing and exploiting core competencies is not new. Channel organizations, such as distributors and sales firms, have been doing just that for decades (actually centuries) — focusing their functional ability across a broad set of products, geographies, and, to a lesser extent, markets. Familiar companies have done the same thing — General Motors, for example, extended its knowl-

12. Mitchell Goozé, (Santa Clara: IMI, 2001), pp. 73–138.

13. C. K. Prahalad and Gary Hamel, (The Core Competence of the Corporation, Harvard Business Review, May–June 1990), pp. 79–81

edge of automobile engine design and manufacture to the train industry by making locomotive engines decades ago.

But there's a difference between General Motors' application of its expertise in the design and manufacture of automobiles to the design and manufacture of trains — something that was not too much of a product or market stretch — and NEC's identification and extension of its semiconductor core competence to other industries. Both companies recognized and exploited a core competency, but NEC extended it to products and markets beyond the obvious.

Extending the industrial era's focus on functional competence to the development and exploitation of a corporation's core competencies across product and market spaces was the crowning post-industrial management achievement. But, while the discipline of core competencies was still on its learning curve, a new, information-stage discipline had already arrived on the horizon.

THE INFORMATION ECONOMY AND THE MANAGEMENT OF CORE PROCESSES

In 1992, Stalk, Evans and Schulman[14] stated that the source of competitive advantage in the future would reside in the management of a corporation's core capabilities — by which they meant its core functional or cross-functional corporate processes.

The concept of a corporate process is inseparable from the dimension of time — the very word *process* implies something in motion. The purpose of a corporate process is to ensure both the completeness of an extensive or complicated activity (or "sufficient completeness," as defined by the competitive environment) and its timeliness. It is thus no coincidence that the identification of a company's core processes as the basis for competitive advantage has arisen in an era when the pace of change has increased dramatically and when the time dimension of the business requires rigorous management.

As Stalk, Evans and Schulman said: "Competition is now a 'war of movement' in which success depends on anticipation of market trends and quick response to changing customer needs.... In such an environment, the essence of strategy is not the structure of the company's products and markets, but the dynamics of its behavior."[15] To this, we are tempted to add the old gunslinger's maxim that

14. George Stalk, Phillip Evans, and Lawrence E. Schulman, "Competing Capabilities: The New Rules of Corporate Strategy," Harvard Business Review, March–April 1992, pp. 57–69

15. Ibid., p. 62

one is either "quick or dead." This is true, but another aphorism from that time must also be borne in mind: "Speed's fine, but accuracy's final." Even in this era of Internet-time, countless high-valued start-ups have found, to their great dismay, that there is still a hard constraint imposed by the need to get it right—from the customers' perspective — before the money runs out.

The pace at which new markets now move — as well as the skills required to serve them and the capital required to fund those who serve them — is not just dramatically faster than ever, but dramatically different in character. In the past, dislocating change tended to occur over the space of a generation or so. Over that amount of time, there was sufficient "give" in the system — in corporations, markets, capital institutions, and labor skills — to respond gracefully to changes in market requirements and to the need for both the new technology and functional skills that defined the baseline necessary for survival. Thus, even as the necessities of corporate survival changed, a competent management was able to respond to them in a timely manner and to hire or develop the people and skills it needed.

The speed of technology and capital movement has now reached the critical velocity whereby change occurs discontinuously. That is, the requirements of the market now change so fast that no amount of refinement to existing corporate competencies allows the corporation to survive the next discontinuity. It is no longer enough to be able to extrapolate — how-ever well — from today's products or markets in order to survive in tomorrow's environment. As is so often said: "It's not that the business is changing, but that change is the business."

Corporations today are serving new customers in new markets with new products. Lean manufacturing (a functional, or even core, competence) means little without the ability to manufacture very *different kinds* of products. Again, Stalk, Evans and Schulman: "As product life cycles accelerate, dominating existing product segments becomes less important than being able to create new products and exploit them quickly."[16]

In-depth knowledge of a market means nothing if a company must serve new markets before it can grow the new crop of management and functional skills necessary to serve the new markets. IBM knew the computer market cold when computers were mainframes and the customer was a large corporate IT department. That knowledge did them little good when consumer and departmental computers (personal computers and mini-computers) came to dominate the mar-

16. Ibid., p. 62

ket and the customer changed. Even a world-class engineering organization is of no use without the ability to integrate different development disciplines. Hewlett-Packard's excellent instrument engineering abilities nearly killed its chances in the laser printer market in its early days, when different engineering practices and a very different development pace were required.[17]

In these cases the problem wasn't that the company couldn't change to meet the requirements of the new environment—it was that it couldn't change in time. The new world was suddenly upon it and it lacked an *inbred mechanism* to discern the trend, assess its import, and respond.

This new economic order — the fourth industrial stage — is often aptly called *the information economy*. This is not to imply that only information and knowledge are of value and traded in this stage. Certainly, information is becoming more and more important in terms of dollars exchanged. But hard manufactured goods— machinery, consumer items, and so on — continue to have great value, too, as they always have and will. Hard goods will be no less important in the information economy than agricultural goods were in the industrial economy.

The term *information economy*, therefore, refers to the *primary* source of competitive advantage in this new era (i.e., information processes), just as the term *industrial economy* reflected the primary source of competitive advantage during its time (industrial efficiency.)

Competitive advantage in the information economy comes from a corporation's ability to gather information, process it, and respond — automatically and nimbly — with appropriate products, services and customer interactions. That is, the information economy is not only about corporate information, but also human *processes*. It assumes an existing set of core and functional competencies to implement the decisions which are the output of these processes.

---

17. Of course, after stumbling, Hewlett-Packard recovered and now dominates this market. This feat is a tribute to the culture and management skills at Hewlett-Packard, which allow it to acknowledge its mistakes and change course quickly. However, even Hewlett-Packard recognized its limitations and split itself into two entities: Agilent and HP.

Period (approx.)	Industrial Stage	Critical Resource	Management Paradigm	Critical Functional Skill	Post-Critical Skill Examples
⟶ 1900	Agrarian	Labor	NA	NA	NA
1900–1950	Industrial	Capital	Functional Competencies	Manufacturing	Quality, JIT
1950–1985				Sales, Promotion	CRM, 1–1, Web Commerce
1985–2000	Post-Industrial	Traditional Managerial Skills	Core Competencies	Product Development	Speed Development Lean Thinking PLM
2000 ⟶	Information	Process Management Skills	Core Processes	Marketing, Innovation, Functional Integration	?

Figure 1-2

STABLE PROCESSES NEEDED IN UNSTABLE MARKETS

Another way to appreciate this new state of affairs is to consider the alignment of the corporation's capabilities and offerings with the market's needs. (Naturally, these two things must be aligned within a profitable company.) Therefore, in order for the company to align itself with a market, it must have a way of referencing its position vis-à-vis the market.

In times of slow market change, the market itself provides its own stable reference. That is, the market is stable enough that a competent observer can easily discern whether or not their company is aligned with it. This means that a company's internal processes for providing products to meet market needs can be unstable, yet the company can still know what the market is doing. It can align itself with the market by observing it and making appropriate corrections.

However, in times of instability and frenetic change, the market does not provide a stable reference to itself, let alone to its future needs. (It is, of course, the future needs of the market we are concerned with, not just its present needs. The future time frame we are concerned with is the time it takes to develop a product — the length of the product development cycle.) In periods of unstable markets, it is only through the use of stable (i.e., rigorous, consistent and accurate) marketing processes that a company can hope to discern the needs of the future market. If the market won't provide its own stable reference, then the enterprise must provide a stable observation point (a stable process) from which to assess it.

38

MARKET

		Stable	Unstable
PROCESSES	**Stable**	Desirable	Necessary
	Unstable	Possible	Impossible

*Unstable markets require
stable corporate processes*

Figure 1-3

Today's overriding reality is that the environment is changing with extreme rapidity. Merely having "good" existing products is approaching irrelevance, because these products have a very limited lifespan. Consider that 80% of HP's and Canon's revenue comes from products less than two years old! We are approaching a time when having a process that tracks the market and keeps the stream of appropriate products flowing will be a baseline competitive competency. Market crises (abrupt changes) *will* inevitably — indeed, regularly do — occur. A company's internal systems and culture must be capable of smoothly incorporating (or better, actually welcoming) them. In this sense, a stable internal marketing process acts like a company's immune system to environmental stresses.

ADVANTAGE INNOVATOR

Since the price of doing business is constantly increasing, it follows that competitive advantage goes to those firms that implement new, useful management processes first. When the telephone was a new device, those firms that installed and used that "new" communications technology gained a competitive advantage for awhile. Likewise with lean thinking — those firms that first implemented this manufacturing tool were at an advantage over their competitors — until their competitors caught on. And those firms in the last decade that have implemented structured product development processes are now competing at a considerable advantage to their less well-managed competitors.

But this advantage only lasts for awhile. Any new source of competitive advantage — be it manufacturing capability in the early part of this century, traditional sales and promotional skills in the Fifties, Sixties, and Seventies, or development of core competencies in manufacturing and/or product development in the Eighties — only provides a short-lived competitive advantage to those who acquire it *first*. Everyone else, of course, must also eventually acquire it, but they do so in catch-up mode.

Competitive advantage, therefore, goes only to the risk takers—to those who pioneer useful new management techniques. Once something is tried-and-true, it is merely another cost of business — not a source of competitive advantage. Another way of saying this is that corporate losers are always a generation or more behind with respect to their management systems.

A corollary to this axiom is that **initial implementations of a new technique are always sub-optimal.** That is, competitive advantage is the result of embarking on a knowingly imperfect initial implementation. The firms that do so, however, have the advantage of honing the new skill while their competitors are just learning it and embarking on their own imperfect initial implementations.

The Principle and Corollaries of Competitive Advantage

- Competitive advantage goes only to the risk takers to those who pioneer useful new management techniques.

- Initial implementations of a new technique are always sub-optimal.

- Gaining competitive advantage is always painful.

Another corollary is that, since competitive advantage is the result of learning something new and different, **gaining competitive advantage is always painful.** It is most painful — if, indeed, possible at all — with companies who must play the catch-up game. A company with a culture and management systems that do not encourage the adoption of useful new management techniques not only loses the competitive advantage of implementing the techniques early, but—when it is eventually forced to adopt them—it is far more painful to do so than for the company in which seeking out new ideas is a part of the culture.

The source of competitive advantage in the frenetic information economy — the new "thing" that differentiates winners from losers — is the corporation's core processes. And the core process that will most differentiate one company from another, as we continue in the new millennium, is the corporation's marketing/sales process. Because, although models and methodologies that aid the company in the development of its core manufacturing and product development processes do exist — indeed, today's best managed companies are already institutionalizing them — no practical models or methods have existed to aid a company in instituting a timely, structured, repeatable process for the entire marketing/sales function.

At least until now.

2

CHAPTER TWO

the missing element

Marketing constitutes half of the integrated marketing/sales process that is addressed in this book. Our belief is that there are sales processes in place in most companies — albeit usually the wrong processes. By contrast, there are very few well-defined marketing processes in the corporate world. Read on and you'll see what we mean by this audacious statement.

Among all corporate functions, marketing alone has the distinction of not having a well-defined process by which it is practiced. All other functions do. Well-established systems, methods, tools and procedures drive manufacturing; likewise with finance, sales, and human resources. Modern accounting processes were developed centuries ago. Even product development — previously a notorious habitat of freewheeling "un-structure" — now has a set of well-ordered processes by which it can be effectively managed. But not marketing.

Marketing suffers from two common misconceptions. The first is the almost ubiquitous confusion of marketing with promotion. Promotion—advertising, publicity, branding, sales support, and so on — is but one area of marketing. Promotion is the "back-end" task of the larger marketing function — the one that is done last in a product's development and introduction cycle. The second universal misconception about marketing is that it's not a science — that it's not something amenable to an organized, structured approach. It is wrongly regarded as an art, as something that is dependent solely on the insight of gifted people for its success.

With these rampant misconceptions in place, is it any surprise that most companies are disappointed with their marketing organization and results?

NO PROCESS

Why is there no well-accepted marketing process today? The first and most obvious answer is that there isn't even a common answer to the question "What is marketing?" Ask 100 managers and marketing practitioners to define marketing and you'll get 150 different answers. How can there be a commonly accepted process for performing a function when there isn't even a commonly agreed upon definition of that function?

The second and most significant answer is that marketing has never been viewed, managed or taught as a process.[18] It has always been viewed, managed and taught in pieces; and, in practice, it has been treated as an art form for which, at best, a company can provide a suitable climate for gifted people.[19] This fragmentation of a discipline that is inherently a process forestalls great strides in its progress.

Discussing economics, Murray Rothbard laments: "Before WWI, the standard method, both of presenting and advancing economic thought, was to write a disquisition setting forth one's vision of the corpus of economic science... Hyper-refinements of detail were generally omitted as impediments to viewing economic science as a whole."[20] The same might today be said of marketing where there is little but hyper-refinement of detail in current advances in the field — as a glance at any academic or even practitioner-level journal will attest.

---

18. The marketing-related Baldridge criteria for performance excellence (www.quality.nist.gov) may appear to be a process-centric approach to marketing, but, from our perspective, these criteria reflect merely an incomplete and loosely linked set of static activities without a true integrating process binding them.

19. Throughout this book, we've borrowed some of the choice phraseology that McGrath, Anthony & Shapiro [Product Development: Success Through Product And Cycle Time Excellence, (Stoneham: Butterworth-Heinemann, 1992)] used to describe the woeful state of Product Development affairs. It's equally applicable to marketing today.

20. Man, Economy and State, vol. 1, (Los Angeles: Nash, 1970), vii.

Of course, it would be impossible to manage marketing as a process without an overall model of the function — one that delineates all of its activities, organizes those activities into manageable sections, and defines the interactions and information flows between those sections and other functional areas. We need the big view — the entire roadmap — otherwise, we get lost in the details. In engineering terms, without an over-arching process model of all of marketing, we can optimize local sub-processes (such as advertising), but are incapable of globally optimizing the system.

The lack of an integrated marketing process has taken its toll on human resources as well. Even as the need for marketing is being recognized, marketing is too often regarded as a backwater for people who aren't bright enough for technical work. This stigma discourages some excellent people from entering into the field and can become a self-fulfilling expectation,[21] one that re-enforces itself through positive feedback. The resulting tension between marketing and product development (typically composed of engineers) only retards the management of marketing as a serious discipline, as well as the integration of marketing and product development.[22]

> ## Why Marketing is Not Managed as a Process
>
> - There is no common definition of "marketing."
>
> - Marketing has never been viewed, managed, or taught as a process.
>
> - Marketing compromises virtually the entire company.
>
> - Most importantly: There has been no over-arching, unified model of the marketing function and process

---

21. Dilbert cartoons aside, this is not meant to suggest that all marketing people are dopes. There are a lot of very bright, energetic people in the function, of course. But they are often frustrated and constrained by the lack of a coherent marketing structure.

22. Of course, one of the success stories of the 1990s has been the increasing involvement of marketing in the new product development (NPD) process. Many studies show a positive relationship between the amount of marketing resources devoted to the NPD process and the resulting product's success. While this relationship must have been the result of more process-like activities occurring in marketing, there is still a long way to go to get to the point where the marketing process is as detailed, complete, and structured as current best-practice NPD processes are today. Still, the success of the increased cooperation between marketing and NPD is an indication of the power of that integration.

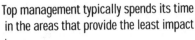

Figure 2-1

Consider the toll that the lack of a well-defined and agreed-upon marketing process takes on the relationship between marketing and sales, which are themselves sister functions in one overall marketing/sales corporate process. The finger pointing and acrimony between marketing and sales — familiar to anyone with any real-world business experience — is inevitable in virtually any company when a new product/service fails to meet expectations. Given that almost every study done of new product success finds that a substantial majority of new products fail, it is no wonder that there is considerable tension between marketing and sales in most companies.

The lack of a unified conceptual framework for marketing means that top management spends little or no time managing marketing as an integrated process. By contrast, they usually spend an inordinate and unproductive amount of time managing the back-end promotional details of marketing, such as trade shows and advertising campaigns. (As a real-world example, we all know CEOs and marketing vice-presidents of major corporations who seem to be frustrated graphic designers, since they spend so much time interfer- ing with the design of promotional materials.) See Figure 2-1.

Reflecing on what Harvard's Steve Wheelwright has pointed out in a product development context, the greatest impact that top management can make on marketing effectiveness is at the front end (opportunity, identification, positioning, etc.) Yet, it depends most of its time on the back-end tasks (promotional tasks and events, sales support, etc.) This is a natural consequence of the fact that there is no unified model of the entire marketing process that would expose these management leverage points. (A properly constructed process would actually

•• Process Mismatch

The XYZ company was a successful publisher of educational materials for industry, health, and non-profit groups. It had grown steadily for over 50 years to become a dominant player in its niche. Market analysis and product development were running as smoothly as a well-oiled machine. The markets and customers were monitored closely by product managers and sales people. Experts in content areas were consulted often. Likewise, the business model and the "numbers" of the business were predictable and well-managed.

Yet the company's existing markets were stagnant, so the decision was made to enter an entirely new business of consulting services to non-profit and government customers. Market entry would be by acquisition. Unfortunately, neither the XYZ company's "front-end" (marketing) or "back-end" (promotion and sales) processes were remotely ready for the task with which they were confronted. Such basic issues as appropriate sales channels and customer buying patterns had not been considered. The inability of the existing sales organization to sell the new services had not been foreseen. The underlying profit model for the new business was utterly different from the existing business, yet the new business was managed though its lens. In short, disaster loomed.

force top management involvement at its highest leverage points.) Top management today spends most of its marketing-related time on the less influential back-end tasks because they are the only ones that are well understood.

Some readers will object: "Aren't there copious examples of real marketing wizards leading companies to profitability — of companies where top management is absolutely engrossed in marketing?"

The answer is, yes, there are, but we must use the word "marketing" with precision. The primary marketing focus of these companies is generally on the back-end sales and promotional aspects of marketing, just as it is in most companies — the difference being that these companies are performing these functions effectively, with focus, and that these companies are at a point in their development where this focus can bring about a blip in sales and profits for a couple of years. In fact, men and women who came up through sales usually lead these companies.

These companies are not really marketing-focused in the holistic, integrated sense of the word; rather, they are promotion and sales focused. The president of IBM (prior to Lou Gerstner) was always a man who had "carried a bag." He was an obvious example of the shortcomings of this practice in today's world. While a focus on the front-end tasks of marketing would have led the company to change course decades earlier, management continued to believe that their problems were due to insufficient effort in the marketing back-end and sales areas.[23]

Yet another reason that marketing is not managed as a process is that marketing, properly defined, is a very big piece of the company. As Peter Drucker says: "Marketing is, first, a central dimension of the entire business. It is the whole business seen from the point of view of its final result, that is, from the customer's point of view. Concern and responsibility for marketing must, therefore, permeate all areas of the enterprise."[24] It is a very large task to bring together all the pieces of marketing, organize them according to a unified model and manage them as an integrated process. It involves large pieces of the enterprise; it requires much change; it challenges existing skills; and it upsets fiefdoms.

But most of all, the reason that marketing isn't managed as an integrated process is because it lacks that integrating, over-arching, defining model.

WHAT MARKETING IS NOT

As we've discussed, marketing is often confused with promotion. But, as befits a function with no commonly agreed-upon definition, marketing is often confused with other things, also. To wit:

All of these problems were predictable and could have been mitigated (and perhaps eliminated) had a true marketing process existed within the company. The processes that were in place were nothing more than the calcification of the "way things were always done," and not a true, live, adaptive process that examined the environment, made strategic decisions about infrastructure and resources, directed product development and aligned sales and promotional activities with them.

The company was essentially caught short by its previous success and its consequent lack of development of a true marketing process. This happens to lots of companies. Recall IBM's early failure to enter the minicomputer market in the 70s, DEC's failures in dismissing the PC market in the 80s, or the U.S. automobile manufacturers dismissing the high-quality subcompact automobile market in the 60s and 70s. • •

---

23. Witness IBM CEO John Aker's leaked memo of 1990 — famous within the computer industry — in which he blamed all the company's troubles on the laziness of the sales force.

24. *People and Performance*, (New York: Harper College Press, 1977) 91.

Marketing Is Not An Art Form. Ninety percent of marketing consists of known, predictable activities. Of course, as in many other professions, ten percent of marketing depends on the originality and insight of its practitioners. In this respect, marketing is like any other professional activity. For example, in the practice of medicine, doctors spend most of their time on routine tasks such as interviewing patients, reading x-rays, performing blood tests, and so on. Performing these routine tasks completely and correctly — according to well-established process guidelines — allows doctors to profitably use the small portion of their time devoted to the non-routine, insight-requiring tasks of diagnosis and treatment selection.

Routine marketing activities include market research, competitive analysis, project management, promotion, and so on. These and other routine[25] marketing activities provide marketing professionals with the "raw material" for the other ten percent of their activities that do require their talent, insight, and experience — analysis and decision-making. The failure of so-called marketing planning software to provide real value — to the extent that it addresses this front-end of marketing sufficiently, which is usually not the case — is that it cannot address that last ten percent.

The key obstacle to achieving this 90/10 state of affairs is that a complete model of marketing, comprising all of its elements and linked by appropriate information flows, is usually missing. Without such a blueprint, both the routine and the non-routine marketing tasks are destined to be performed incompletely and without integration. When this occurs, marketing just drifts, without structure, according to the needs of the moment and the predilections of the person directing it.

Marketing Is Not Sales. Marketing and sales are integrated and related, but they are different. They compose the single, integrated corporate function of marketing/sales; but, although they overlap, they are distinct functions. Regarding them as the same thing causes a plethora of problems. Marketing is concerned first with selecting and understanding the customers and what those customers value, while sales is primarily concerned with how customers want to buy. From a time-frame perspective, marketing consists of both operational and strategic activities, while sales is more of an operational, quarter-to-quarter function. Marketing horizons may look forward two, five, or even more years, while sales horizons seldom exceed one year.

---

25. Certainly these tasks require creativity and intelligence; the point here is that their methodologies are well known.

This difference can be clearly seen in the kinds and amounts of effort needed to improve these functions. Making a corporation truly marketing-driven, or tightly forging links between marketing and product development, often requires the re-making of the company's entire culture and processes. By contrast, beefing up sales is something that can be done in a *relatively* short amount of time by hiring more salespeople, effective sales training,[26] or funding demand enhancement campaigns.

What Marketing is Not

- Marketing is not an art form.

- Marketing is not sales.

- Marketing is not promotion.

- Marketing is not the "Four P's"

Marketing Is Not Promotion. Say "marketing" to most people and they will immediately think of advertising, trade shows, publicity, and other kinds of promotion. Yet promotion is only one of several major marketing areas. In the comprehensive model of marketing/sales detailed later, marketing will include several major tactical areas and a major strategic (or planning) area. *Promotion*, which overlaps with sales, is but one of these areas; and, while requiring considerable talent to do effectively, it is currently the best understood of all of them. Lack of effective promotional know-how is not usually the problem!

Marketing Is Not The "Four P's." In *Basic Marketing*,[27] the classic introductory text, which has influenced generations of business students, E. Jerome McCarthy came up with the term the "Four P's" — product, place, price and promotion — as a way to remember the basic elements of the marketing mix. He never intended this term, or its components, to be a complete description of the entire marketing function. Nevertheless, catchy phrases have great appeal. Today, many in management still believe that the "Four P's" are all there is to marketing.

The contextual value of the "Four P's" is better reflected in a marketing/sales process model where the "Four P's" compose the positioning activities within sub-areas of the marketing planning element of the model.

---

26. It is our belief that much of today's sales training is either extremely elementary (which is the appropriate training where it is) or simply wrong.

27. Basic Marketing: A Managerial Approach, 5th ed., (Homewood: Irwin, 1975) 75.

EVERY SYSTEM IS ALREADY PERFECTLY CONSTRUCTED (TO ACHIEVE THE RESULTS IT'S GETTING)

Most human, and almost all corporate, activities are so complex that they require some sort of model to organize and manage them coherently. Marketing is no different. In the next-quarter-focused world of poorly run businesses, the notion of a "model" often elicits an immediate negative reaction. "We don't care about *theory*," the reaction goes, "we are concerned with *practical* actions." This attitude is both absurd and illogical.

The whole reason we develop models is to expose the underlying principles of surface phenomena and to reveal their true structure, thus making it possible to *understand* and *manage* them. The principles of chemistry and models of chemical reactions make it easier for us to manage chemical processes than if we were proceeding by trial and error. If we want to train a dog to perform a task, that training will be much more effective if we have a model describing the way a dog learns. If we want to build a house, we need a blueprint. In fact, the most practical action we can take is to begin with a model.

The disadvantages of having no organized, structured approach to marketing are legion. And, what's worse, they permeate the entire enterprise. Anyone who has spent even a little time in an organizational setting will recognize the following problems. Each of them can be traced to the lack of a defined marketing process.

Marketing seems to change with every new regime. With each new marketing director or vice president, the marketing function is reorganized; resource allocation is completely rearranged; new activities are introduced, while various long-established activities are trashed; no process for rational decision-making is put in place. The new management brings in people with backgrounds similar to their own—a market researcher brings in market research people; a former sales executive brings in field people; a financial manager brings in lots of financial types. As a result, certain marketing activities are overemphasized, while other necessary activities are ignored. This constant organizational shuffling, by never establishing complete, coherent and integrated marketing practices, allows ineffective behaviors to become institutionalized.

There is a new definition of marketing every time the company gets in trouble. One time it's "customer closeness," another time it's "strategic positioning," another time it's "branding." A serious discussion of the role of marketing — let alone the implementation of a rational process approach to it — always seems to be usurped by the "more pressing" (in reality, the more understandable) immediate issues, which are often driven by a short-term lack of sales.

There is no consistency over time or across products. There is no common language for the elements of marketing and their inter-relationships. There are no defined marketing decision points. There is no way to characterize a marketing process and no way to discover best practices within it. Organizational learning is stymied and, without a defined process, there can be no process improvement and no climbing the learning curve.

Each new product introduction or market entry requires management to spend countless hours figuring out what the marketing will be this time. Whatever bit of structure marketing had instituted last time was specific to that situation, so it is now deemed invalid. One of the most frequent questions in this situation is: "What is marketing anyway?" No such confusion exists in other well-defined functions. No one asks, "What is manufacturing?" or "What is finance?" or "What is sales?" Certainly, there are many debates about the best way to perform these functions, but there is little confusion about their basic natures and their fundamental activities.

The ability to justify resources doesn't exist. When an engineering manager or a sales manager requests additional resources, they have little trouble specifying exactly which activities will get done and the results that can be expected. Marketing managers, on the other hand, are often at a loss to tie an obviously necessary activity to corporate profitability or some intermediate goal.

Without a defined process, marketing tends to lurch from one crisis to another. In this state, marketing is consistently reacting to market dynamics rather than *anticipating* them. One of the insidious organization behaviors this atmosphere engenders is an ever-increasing focus on internal issues and politics, rather than an external-market focus.

Marketing is hardly a smoothly running ship. All corporate functions have their cells of ineffectiveness and irrelevance. But, with no unified process in place to identify the necessary activities and to integrate them, marketing seems to harbor more than others. Marketing coordination with other functions — particularly product development — is notoriously poor. Without even a static structure in place to characterize the function, let alone a dynamic process that integrates it with other functions (and the outside world), this is no surprise.

Without a structured process that demands decisions at specific points, there are fatal delays in decision-making. An ad-hoc decision making process is a reflection of an overall ad-hoc marketing process. Decisions are pushed up or aside, rather than being forced at the appropriate time and place by the appropriate people at the lowest possible level. Decision responsibility is not defined and inadequate information is provided to support it.

Marketing is organized in a seemingly random fashion. Tasks and responsibilities overlap and there are critical gaps between them. The information necessary for informed decision-making is not specified and is not gathered. The flow of information to appropriate people and teams, and its proper processing, doesn't happen. Inter-functional communication (again, particularly with product development and sales) is ineffective, if it exists at all. Marketing becomes a collection of fiefdoms, rather than an integrated set of coherent activities, and inappropriate skill sets are hired into the function.

There are no objective criteria for measuring the effectiveness of marketing. (We are reminded of one large company, which, frustrated by this very fact, officially declared that it would measure marketing by its "obvious quality." We are not making this up — the people promulgating this

Problems Caused by the Lack of a Unified Marketing Process

- "Marketing" changes with each new regime.

- "Marketing" changes at each crisis.

- There is no marketing consistency across time and products.

- Each new product introduction causes a "reinvention" of marketing.

- Marketing has no ability to justify resources.

- Marketing lurches from one crisis to another.

- Marketing does not run smoothly.

- There are fatal delays in decision-making.

- Marketing is organized randomly.

- There is no objective marketing measurement criteria.

were senior and presumably sober corporate executives) Naturally, without a way to define and measure marketing, continuous improvement in the function is impossible.

Short-term "marketing successes" often hide fatal structural flaws in the system. And, while marketing failures are easy to identify, fixing the underlying structural problems is impossible without an overall model of that structure. As a corollary, there is no rational way to measure the performance of marketing individuals involved in critical front-end activities, such as opportunity identification. Often these people are simply evaluated on the basis of present sales!

FAD APPROACHES AND PARTIAL VISION

Management is usually aware of the crisis in marketing, but, without a unified model of the function, they are at a loss to do much about it. As a result, there are a lot of fads that pass for marketing panaceas. Such recent fascinations as "branding" and "integrated marketing" (which, in reality, means only "integrated marketing communications") are worthwhile (even necessary) elements of a complete marketing process in and of themselves. But sold as a cure-all, they often become another fad-of-the-year. We saw evidence of this in an article in *Advertising Age* that proposed creating the position of Chief Branding Officer. Even an elementary review of the responsibilities of this position revealed a total overlap with the role of Chief Marketing Officer.

Fads are merely quick-fix tactical programs (that sometimes fix very little), usually concentrating on the more easily grasped back-end promotional side of marketing and often selected on the basis of popular buzzwords. These concepts, however well designed and implemented, and however necessary in an overall scheme of things, do nothing to fix, let alone erect, an overall marketing process. They cause the company to spend a lot of time on some fairly low-level marketing activities, and many other — often more important — marketing areas are neglected and begin to atrophy. Since a chain is only as strong as its weakest link, the company winds up "behinder" than before. These fads typically provide some focus to an already too-narrow marketing management span of attention. But they do not expand it.

The marketing situation of most companies today can be likened to a house constructed without a frame. Imagine a house built without any (or very few) studs, joists, and beams, with the plasterboard panels tacked only to each other and jerry-rigged in place. Such a house would be extremely fragile and constantly in need of repair. Each little jolt would destroy entire sections of it. Is it advisable for the owners to spend their time and money on surface repairs such as new windows (branding) and new bath fixtures (integrated marketing)? Or is it not a more intelligent course of action to first erect a sturdy frame for the house? Unfortunately, in their desire for a quick-fix, too many otherwise intelligent people erect their marketing structure on woefully inadequate designs.

Those designs are often based on superficial changes. It would be like trying to structurally integrate one of those old New England farmhouses, that are composed of several different structures concatenated together over generations, by doing nothing more than siding the whole complex with a single color of siding. Of course, residing the whole thing may give the appearance of one house, but that's just an illusion. There are still incompatible structural, plumbing, and heating systems underneath. Unless the whole structure is evaluated — and intelligently, at that — the surface "re-engineering" is likely to cause more problems than it solves, as anyone who has ever dabbled in restoration, or lived through a faddish re-engineering effort can attest.

The quick fix is simply not the answer.

In this book, we argue the case for a structured, unified marketing/sales model as the basis of a unified marketing/sales process, and describe objective methods to manage the process. We then present an overview of the first instance of a practical integrated marketing/sales model. Finally, we'll demonstrate how universal management methods that have been applied successfully to the manufacturing side of the business apply equally well to marketing/sales.

With this book you can leave behind the fads and quick fixes to marketing and sales, and begin to build a *sustaining* competitive advantage based on the process that is at the irreducible core of your business: connecting your customers needs with your capabilities.

3

CHAPTER THREE

how to manage your company for value acceleration

T he notion of corporate processes has come under a great deal of criticism in recent years. "There's just no time to do things in the old-fashioned, step-at-a-time way in a NetSpeed economy," the argument runs, "Instead of 'ready, aim, fire' — or even Tom Peters' famous, 'ready, fire, aim' — there's no time to aim. It's come down to 'fire, change, and fire again.'"

With this mentality, any attention to process seems irrelevant and passé. For many, the very word process brings to mind the lumbering, slothful bureaucracies that are dead or dying in the 21st Century.

PROCESS IS STILL ESSENTIAL

We beg to differ. In fact, we believe that effective corporate processes are eternally essential — and more so the faster the rate of change.

The meltdown of the hyper-inflated Internet stocks in 2000 confirms our belief in process. In the earlier period of Internet stock insanity, essentially free money was available to anyone with a skimpy plan and venture backing. That is no longer a viable strategy and we are witnessing the return to valid business models, backed by actual, reachable markets with valuable products or services. Wall Street is expecting that all this will be backed up by experienced professionals with the ability to implement the business in a sustainable way. The essential necessity of business basics—including processes—survives.

THE NATURE OF PROCESS

If process is so essential to the success of a company, it's important that we understand exactly what is meant by the term. What is a "process?" A process is something that defines and orders a set of activities. Whether it defines them in terms of outcomes or specific actions performed (a distinction to be discussed later) is not important. The relevant point is that a process assigns roles and responsibilities to people or units and defines the information flows between them. A process ensures that everyone knows their jobs and how what they do integrates with what others do. The alternative is to have no means by which to differentiate essential activities from non-essential ones. As a result, activities are done chaotically and randomly. Clearly, that is not productive, nor is it what the opponents of corporate process are arguing for.

Of course, any given process can be poorly defined or well-defined, healthy or malignant, effective or not. Much of the resistance to processes is clearly a reaction to their misuse — to processes gone amuck, to processes mired in bureaucracy, and to processes composed of "no-ops." But the fact is that without organizing processes, a corporation dies a death of entropy — something we have seen all to often.

Effective managers have always known that you manage by process — and, further, that the job of management is to define and manage the processes that are

•• Intuit Discovers Process

Intuit is a software company well known for it's Quicken personal finance, Turbotax, and QuickBooks packages, all of which absolutely dominate their product categories. Yet in 2000, it was a company in disarray. One of its key profit centers had virtually no documented procedures, was losing money, and had stone-age slow execution. Intuit was 20 years old. What had begun as an obsessive, user-friendly culture had devolved into a consensus-hamstrung bureaucracy. They had found that focusing exclusively on current customer needs was no way to get the early, critical foothold in new markets. As a result, they had become a slow, indecisive company that had missed several opportunities that would have played to their brand and strengths.

When Steve Bennett, a 23-year veteran of GE's process-driven culture, arrived as Intuit's new CEO, he immediately installed a process culture. As at GE, Mr. Bennett used the Six Sigma methodology as the process template for measurement and change. Tough, zero-based budgeting processes were installed; an objective-driven compensation process was initiated; and even the notorious anti-process software development culture became process-driven at Intuit.

New market initiatives were the result of a process approach for strategy and market selection. Intuit expanded its accounting offerings to small businesses of all sizes and capitalized on the opportunity for efficient, user-friendly ERP-like integrated suites for companies with less than 250 employees. And the results have been impressive, with customers and developers signing on, Intuit's revenues expanding at a double-digit rate, and operating margins nearly doubling — all since process excellence has become the management mantra. ••

essential to the enterprise. That is to say, the job of management is to define those processes that are necessary, to organize those processes in a logical way, and to link corporate processes together synergistically. Paraphrasing Stephan H. Haeckel, "Processes are the means by which organizational capabilities produce their outcomes."[28] Haeckel refers to the linking of business processes as "systems design." A process can be specified to have short or long decision time-frames and can operate with a greater or lesser amount of decision certainty — the appropriate specification of the process' operating parameters is the job of management.

Michael Hammer, who is easily recognized as the father of the re-engineering movement, points out that "it is important to realize that companies moving to process-centering do not create or invent their process-

> **"Effective CEOs use process to drive decisions, not delay them."**
>
> "Why CEOs Fail," Fortune, June 21, 1999, 76

es. The processes have been there all along, producing the company's outputs."[29] Without a company performing its critical activities to some minimal extent, the

28. Adaptive Enterprise: Creating and Leading Sense-and-Respond Organizations, (Cambridge: Harvard Business School Press, 1999) 275.

29. Beyond Reengineering, (New York: HarperBusiness, 1996) 10, 29. Note: Reengineering — the valid and necessary focus on identifying, organizing around and managing one's core business processes — has suffered the ignominious fate that also befell the TQM movement — another fundamentally valid management practice. While pointing out that these two practices never actually ceased in well-managed companies, but are fundamentally necessary, Dr. A. Blanton Godrey in his Foreword to The Process-Centered Enterprise (Boca Raton: St. Lucie Press, 1999) iv, offers several reasons for the perceived "failure" of process-centered reengineering in companies that are not well-managed. Key among these is that these companies try to buy reengineering from an outside firm. They do not make the commitment to undertaking this fundamental shift of business focus upon themselves and, thus, they abdicate one of the real jobs of management. Godfrey also points out that "Without the fundamental ideas of quality management being well understood and practiced in an organization, the organization does not have the tools to manage [its] critical processes."(Ibid, iv) For more on this, we direct the reader to Chapter 6 on managing a true marketing/sales process.

company would cease to exist. This is true whether we are talking about business processes or functional processes. What the NetSpeed economy has done, however, is to hasten the rate at which companies and business units — indeed entire business models — can suddenly die. "Everyone is watching out for task performance, but no one has been watching to see if all the tasks together produce the results they're supposed to…"[30]

If ever there was a description of the current state of affairs in marketing, this is it! Most firms can point to marketing activities and tasks that are done well — perhaps even at a world-class level. So why do most of these same firms suffer from the symptoms of ineffective overall marketing? It's because these excellently executed marketing activities are not linked together and with other corporate functions into an effective marketing *process.*

The NetSpeed argument against process is founded on the maxims that the pace of change is frenetic, that near real-time decision making is required, and that we no longer have time to do things perfectly the first time. All true. But all this means is that the processes that allow a company to prosper in a NetSpeed environment must be designed around these realities. It is perfectly possible to design processes that are rapid-reacting and that correct for imperfection the first time.

30. Hammer, Beyond Re-engineering, 11.

31. Kayte Vanscoy, "Unconventional Wisdom," 78-88

•• Dot-coms Discovers Process

In October of 2000, Smart Business pointed out that "one startup after another has been riddled by the sorts of mistakes that business schools have been railing against for half-a-century: entering markets with too many competitors; throwing good money after bad; and most of all, an appalling lack of planning." The article, ironically titled "Unconventional Wisdom," went on to say that, although strategic planning and theoretical frameworks "may not have the drama of making a big splash with your IPO … they still matter." In fact, despite initial skepticism, the arrival of the Internet had only served to strengthen the importance of traditional marketing concepts. One fresh undergrad, who had survived a few years at a dot-com before heading off to business school was quoted as saying: "I didn't have a good foundation in business knowledge to make the decisions I was making. It was all trial and error." Not surprisingly, she went on to explain that there had been no processes in place at the dot com to get things done correctly.[31] ••

Combat military procedures are dramatic examples of these kinds of processes and they have been in use for a very long time. Even under the real-time, life-and-death constraints of combat, plans and procedures are still essential to a unit's success. While the procedures of a relatively fixed-mission organization, such as the infantry, may be relatively inflexible, the processes of dynamic Special Warfare units are designed to adapt to a rapidly changing environment — but they are processes nonetheless.

> **"In volatile markets, corporate strategy should focus on process..."**
>
> Kathleen M. Eisenhardt and Sharon L. Brown, "Patching" (Harvard Business Review. May – June 1999)

The same is true of a hospital trauma unit. Things happen fast and unpredictably there — much faster than at any company — but trauma units are successful at saving lives because they are experts at implementing clearly defined, emergency diagnostic and medical processes. Often, the procedures under execution must change suddenly, but that change in sub-processes (procedures) is an adaptive element in the larger process of treating the patient's injuries ... and one that first-rate teams excel at executing.

One last example: imagine a basketball team with no assigned positions and no plays practiced before a game. This would be a dysfunctional team indeed! Yet the new-age, network-economy, flat-organization, don't-plan-beyond-next-week hoopla espoused by the popular business press would have you believe that that is the right way to run a company.

The fact is, even though a basketball game is completely unpredictable even seconds in advance, there are defined roles and responsibilities for the players and defined processes (plays) that must be mastered in order to be successful in that chaotic environment.

UNSTABLE MARKETS REQUIRE STABLE PROCESSES

This brings us back to the diagram from page 20 (See Figure 3-1).

Figure 3-1

As the NetSpeed economy presents us with an increasingly frenetic market, as decisions must be made in shorter and shorter time-frames, and as the importance of doing *something* within your market window becomes more important than doing it *perfectly*, corporate processes will be more important than ever. In an economy in which customers are fickle and product lives are shorter than their development time, it is no exaggeration to say that a company will actually be defined by its *processes* rather than its *products*. That is, a company will be defined by what it is capable of doing—by the capability of its processes — rather than what it has made.

In times of frenetic change, *adaptation* must be a defined characteristic of all corporate processes. Each process must include the feedback mechanisms that change the process itself based on the changes in the environment and the results the process is generating.

We can view corporate processes as the internal "plumbing" of an enterprise. If your house lies in a flood area and floods come only occasionally, with plenty of warning — that is, your environment is fairly stable — then the plumbing in your house that responds to flooding can be in slip-shod shape. In this stable environment, you will have plenty of time to know when a flood is coming, and you will be able to shore up your inadequate plumbing with temporary fixes to handle the water. But, if floods come often and without warning—if your environment is unstable — then you will need well-thought-out, competent and well-maintained plumbing to survive each flood.

FUNCTIONAL VS. BUSINESS PROCESSES

Recall this from earlier:

> *The process-centric corporation of the future will be made up of many inter-locking processes — some functional and some cross-functional. Indeed, the success of cross-functional corporate processes will stand on the foundation of strong functional skills and processes.*
>
> *This last point is still not well understood. With all of the (deserved) attention that business processes — which are almost always necessarily cross-functional — have gotten in the past decade, it's all too easy to forget that functional skills are the basis of these cross-functional processes.*

Even now, in the literature of business process, there is little appreciation of this critical point. We referred earlier to product development — a critical cross-functional business process in almost any enterprise. Yet it is still common for even world-class product development processes to fail to produce products (or services) that sell well and are profitable. The reason is clear to anyone who's seen this happen in real life and it goes by the old computer term "GIGO" — garbage in, garbage out. That is, unless marketing — a functional member of the cross functional product development team — can hold up its end of the bargain — can reliably identify a market and a product that will serve that market — then all the product development capability in the world is useless. And marketing is a functional discipline.

This can be seen more clearly if we consider the functional discipline of engineering. Engineering is a specific functional area in a company and the processes by which engineers design products must, obviously, be defined and efficient in an effective company. Now try to imagine an engineering department running without any design and test processes, an engineering department dependent only on the whims of individual engineers, and — well, it's impossible to imagine! Crisp engineering processes are part of what make possible an effective cross-functional product development process.

Therefore, business processes stand on the foundation of strong functional capabilities, and these functional capabilities are best rendered by process of their own. Some examples of this relationship are depicted in Figure 3-2.

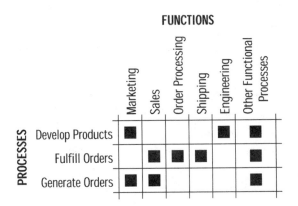

Figure 3-2

This is a straightforward functional/process matrix, similar to ones that you have undoubtedly seen many times before. But it accurately depicts the relationship of business processes to functional processes. (Whether each business process "owns" their own autonomous functional process or whether they share functional expertise with other processes is not relevant to this point — although it is a vital organizational design consideration.) The point here is that business processes are composed of functional disciplines (and "white space" management) — and that each of these functional disciplines had better have its own well-defined process by which it runs in order for the overall business process to be effective.

The characteristic of adaptiveness is a critical one for any effective overall functional (or business) process to have. Pall[32] argues that any process lies somewhere along an axis that depicts its amount of pre-determination, with entirely ad-hoc processes at one end of the axis and entirely known procedures at the other. Given the amount of unpredictability in today's markets, it's clear that any business process must contain a certain amount of adaptability (must be at least somewhat ad-hoc). And when we consider the nature of a marketing process — a process that tracks the environment and guides the company in responding to it—it's very clear that such a process must support a great deal of ad-hoc activity; that is,

---

32. Gabriel A. Pall, *The Process Centered Enterprise: The Power of Commitments*, Boca Raton, FL, St. Lucie Press, 2000, page vi

33. Ibid

it must be highly adaptive. This is the point made above when referring to sports teams, special military units and trauma units. Since these environments are unpredictable, the processes must be ad-hoc and adaptive, but without a process orientation nothing useful will be accomplished — indeed, chaos will result.

Pall makes a further distinction between procedural and ad-hoc processes.[33] He asserts that procedural (pre-determined) processes specify *what* happens at each step in the process, while an ad-hoc process specifies *who owes what to whom at each step.* That is, a procedural process is about activities, while an ad-hoc process is about commitments. The management of a procedural process likewise consists of managing the correct performance of activities, while the management of an ad-hoc process consists of monitoring and facilitating commitments among units or people.

This distinction is a useful one, but possibly confusing in real-life, since all processes — living as they do along the scale between these two poles — have characteristics of both types. In the model of marketing and sales described in the following chapters, we take a different, but complementary, approach: we specify the information that flows from one element of the process model to another. The model is thus constructed as an information flow model because we believe the marketing/sales process is simpler to manage when viewed in that way—with the tools that we believe are best suited to manage a complex human process.

PROCESS AND THE ADAPTIVE ENTERPRISE

For all of the hoopla, books and articles that have been written over the last decade describing — or purporting to describe — the shift in the economy, in business models, and in corporate management as a result mainly of the Internet, one of the most insightful and sustainable contributions has been the work cited earlier by Stephan Haeckel in his book, *Adaptive Enterprise: Creating and Leading Sense-and-Respond Organizations.* That book and the ideas presented in it may seem to present a powerful argument against a process orientation; but, on closer reflection, we believe otherwise.

It is the assertion of that book that the old "make and sell" organizations of the industrial age cannot survive in an environment in which it is impossible to predict the future. Haeckel maintains that the old notion of a firm, viewed as a collec-

---

34. Haeckel, Adaptive Enterprise, xviii

tion of competencies around which management planned and executed business strategy, is simply unworkable in the information age. His thesis is that, in an unpredictable environment, planned responses are, obviously, unworkable. He goes so far to say that "corporate strategy collapses into a universal imperative: become a complex adaptive system"[34]— that is, become a "sense and respond" organization. Stated another way, corporate strategy shifts from the process of reconciling a company's mission, resources, competencies and market needs, to the construction of an organism that is capable of real-time sensing of customer's needs and real-time responses to them.

Taken out of context and taken literally—as will no doubt be done by many commentators — this thesis may seem to imply that any sort of planning or process orientation within a company is worse than unnecessary. Let us examine a few of the reasons that this is not so.

While real-time sensing of market trends and desires is possible, real-time responses are usually not. The quickness with which a firm can respond to a market change — leaving aside the entire logistics issue of getting a product or service into the hands of a customer — is clearly dependent on how long it takes to make the product or service. That is, the product development cycle is the limiting factor (assuming instantaneous delivery) on a firm's response time. If we are talking about changing a POS display at an end-cap in a supermarket, then the response time can be fairly quick — it requires only that the manufacturer's local representative rearrange the display. And while this change of display is theoretically a different "product," by any measure of common sense, it is a trivial one in the absurd extreme.

If, however, we are talking about developing, an entirely new class of high-performance computer, then we are introducing a phase lag between the sensing of market needs and product availability — no matter how efficient and effective the product development function is. In this latter, more substantial (and societally valuable) case, the unavoidable phase lag necessitates the need for the traditional tools of market research, strategy, and prediction.

Now, it's important to realize that both examples above are examples of sense-and-respond organizations. Understanding what your customers need (or will need) and then developing a product/service that meets those needs in the appropriate time frame is what successful businesses are all about. Viewed in this light *only*, the sense-and-respond thesis seems to offer nothing new. Indeed, it is interesting to note that the examples of sense-and-respond organizations that Haeckel cites in his book are in businesses that essentially create products out of thin air—most frequently, financial instruments.

But, ultimately, someone has to make the *stuff* we need! Someone has to make our clothes, our houses, our automobiles and our medicines. And some of this stuff is complicated and time-consuming to make. If we look to the new Internet success stories that are "re-inventing" the way business is done and have "obliterated the old business models," we find that, in most cases, while a new business model may have supplanted an older one, the change has been in the procurement mechanism of physical goods (including services) or the procurement and delivery of bits (information.) That is, it's only been a matter of rearranging how the electrons flow!

Now, lots of good and lots of economic efficiency have come from this burst of Internet commerce activity—including speeding up the time in which stuff is designed and made. But what we've witnessed (and will witness for awhile) is the one-time replacement of a time delay in information transmission with near-instantaneous transmission. There will always be elements in the making of complex products that simply take time — people can only think so fast and machines have limitations. So, therefore there are limits on how much of the economy can forego their traditional management tools of strategic thinking and implementation.

Our thesis is that the sense-and-respond organization will not replace more traditionally managed organizations completely. We believe that all organizations, depending on their product development time, the complexity of their products, and the instability of their environments, exist somewhere along an axis — with pure real-time sense-and-respond organizations at one pole and the traditionally managed organization at the other, and most, some mix of the two. We also believe that information technology is constantly pushing most organizations closer to the sense-and-respond pole over time.

Indeed, Haeckel's book does not take the simplistic view that we allude to above. He recognizes that there are limits to an organization's response time and he understands that an organization's capabilities and competencies have to form limits on the content of any response. His book is worthwhile and provides deep insight into the new ways of organizing and managing that are required, as all organizations become more sense-and-respond like — oriented toward rapid response.

However, the sense-and-response argument that Haeckel describes should not be simplistically used as a reason not to take responsibility for process design and implementation.

So where does this leave process in a sense-and-respond organization? Actually, it leaves it in the same place as in any organization. Processes are the means by which things get done ... pure and simple. Without process, you have chaos. It is processes — notably a marketing process — that form the sensing mechanism of a sense-and-respond organization. It is processes that compose the response mechanisms of a sense-and-respond organization. Processes form the foundation of any enterprise — sense-and-respond, make-and-sell, or anything in between.

PART *2* TWO

EQUIPPING YOUR COMPANY FOR VALUE ACCELERATION

4

C H A P T E R F O U R

could you "manufacture" customers?

MARKETING/SALES HAVE BEEN LEFT BEHIND

The great strides in management over the last 100 years have been the result of the systematic analyses of business processes and the development of proven management techniques and intervention technologies. Perhaps the greatest strides have been made in the manufacturing arena, although other business functions — finance, engineering, human resources, and so on — have also benefited.

But marketing and sales have not. These two overlapping functions continue to be managed, for the most part, by the same "seat of the pants" methods that they always have been. While it's true that certain sub-areas of the marketing and sales functions are now truly analytical (data mining and market research, for example), the entire functions still lack truly rigorous management.

This lack of progress in the marketing/sales area is an inevitable result of two fundamental deficiencies:

1. The lack of a complete, over-arching, integrated, detailed model of the two functions.

2. The lack of proven management methods in marketing/sales.

71

Without a complete, over-arching model of these functions, there can be no true understanding of them, no grasp of the sub-functions that compose them (and their relationship to each other), and no systematic analysis of them. Certainly, there can be no application of proven management methods to marketing/sales if there is no understanding of these functions at a detailed systems level.

APPLYING "MANUFACTURING" PRINCIPLES TO MARKETING/SALES

What if you considered marketing/sales as a manufacturing process and considered the output of this manufacturing process to be loyal, profitable customers? That perspective would allow the application of rigorous manufacturing-based management methods to this new "Customer Manufacturing" process. Why manufacturing-based management methods? Because these methods are not, in fact, manufacturing-specific. Instead, they apply to any well-defined process and they have proven themselves as practical, effective management methodologies over the last 50 years.

How are product manufacturing and marketing/sales similar? Both are processes that take raw material, transform it, and output a desired good. Specifically, marketing/sales takes a market need (raw material), provides value-added goods or services (the transformation), and produces loyal, profitable customers.

Marketing/Sales is further like manufacturing in that each of these functions can be managed as a set of work-cells with raw material as input to the cell, work-in-progress (WIP) within each cell, and finished goods as output of the cell. In a lead qualification work-cell within the sales process, for example, the work-cell input may be a lead, the WIP, or value-add within the cell, may be the conversation that the salesperson has with the prospect, and the work-cell's output is the decision of the salesperson about what to do next with the prospect.

Likewise, in a market research process, the understanding of competitive pricing may be an individual work-cell. Here the inputs are the data gathered from the press, web sites, the sales force, and so on; the WIP is the analysis of this data to discern trends and meaning; and the output consists of reports and recommendations to other work-cells within sales strategy and market positioning.

Like a series of manufacturing work-cells, each marketing/sales work-cell has scrap rates, yields, quality measures, and latencies. Viewing marketing/sales in an integrated, work-cell-like fashion thus allows time-proven process management principles to be applied to the management of the system.

Engineering/Production is now an integrated process in well-managed companies. Marketing/Sales needs to become a well-integrated process too. In fact, marketing is to sales what engineering is to production. Just as in the manufacturing process, where design errors create headaches for production, any deficiencies in marketing will inevitably manifest themselves as problems for sales.

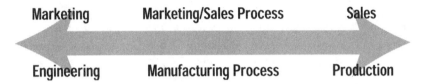

Marketing   **Marketing/Sales Process**   **Sales**

Engineering   **Manufacturing Process**   **Production**

Figure 4-1

For example, in the "old" days, if your production line was producing faulty goods, you'd go to the production manager and scream at him (it was usually a "him" back then), in the belief that your production quality would improve. Back then, it never occurred to you that the reason that the production lines were having trouble producing "good" stuff was that the design of those items might be faulty. It may have simply been a bad design, or maybe it was a good, but not a manufacturable, design.

Now, as silly as this sounds today in a manufacturing context, we nonetheless still see the same thing going on in a marketing/sales context. Today, if sales are off, you tend to hunt down your sales manager and flog him or her in the belief that that's how you cause sales to improve. Yet the real problem causing sales to be down may be that the groundwork for those sales — done by marketing — is faulty, or that marketing specified an un-sellable product. In *The Secret to Selling More*,[35] Mitch focuses in detail on this subject.

A COMPLETE MARKETING/SALES MODEL

A model is a description of a set of activities that orders and makes sense of them. Both marketing and sales are composed of hundreds of individual tasks and activities. This inherent complexity, coupled with the long-standing feeling that these functions are more art than science, has led most companies to manage their marketing and sales functions on an event or project basis (or even on a crisis basis.) To be managed effectively, however, marketing/sales must be *managed as a process.*[36]

35. Mitchell Goozé, (Santa Clara: IMI 2001), 73-138

A useful process model provides three main benefits:

- It delineates and orders all of the activities of marketing/sales in a structured hierarchical manner; as such, it allows you to build a marketing/sales process that is *comprehensive*—with nothing falling through the cracks (indeed, without any cracks.)

- It defines the information flows between the elements and sub-elements of the process; thus ensuring that marketing/sales is an *integrated* function, and that the information it operates on is *complete* and *accurate*.

- It allows the marketing/sales process to be managed with the methods that have proven so successful on the manufacturing floor.

HOW DOES A USEFUL MARKETING/SALES PROCESS MODEL WORK?

A useful marketing/sales process model based on the manufacturing metaphor takes an existing set of ad-hoc marketing and sales activities, and transforms them into a reliable, repeatable System to Manufacture Customers.[37] This is accomplished in several steps. The first is to structure marketing/sales as a series of work-cells, using the Customer Manufacturing System process model as a design template from which a company-specific System to Manufacture Customers is produced. This is generally accomplished in chalk-board or brown-paper sessions with corporate management and marketing and sales management after an in-depth assessment of a company's existing marketing and sales activities.

The second is to measure and manage the individual work-cells, as well as the overall Customer Manufacturing plant with appropriate techniques. Note that we put "measure" before "manage." You can't manage what you can't measure — a lesson that the production floor has learned painfully over the last few decades. Just like a series of manufacturing work-cells, at each marketing/sales work-cell you will have scrap rates, yields, quality rates, and time delays. Acceptable measures for each of these must be determined. After capturing this data over time,

36.   Recall that we believe that an information-flow based process description is the approach best suited to managing real-world marketing/sales systems.

37. The term Customer Manufacturing System refers to our process model for manufacturing customers. The term System to Manufacture Customers refers to a specific concrete instantiation of the Customer Manufacturing System. In other words, using the Customer Manufacturing System, a company can create its own System to Manufacture Customers.

you can then manage each work-cell, and the overall marketing/sales process, with the process principles of *lean thinking, constraint analysis*, and *continuous improvement*. These are not just manufacturing-specific management tools — rather they are process management tools. These techniques apply equally well to a well-defined marketing/sales process as to a manufacturing process.

For example, quality control is a foundational competence for any modern manufacturing organization, and it's thoroughly incorporated into the production operations of competitive businesses. Marketing/Sales, however, has been resistant to the application of TQM. The reason is simple — you can't maintain quality control of a process if you can't describe the elements (work-cells) of the process, and precisely define the required inputs, desired outputs and in-process criteria of those work-cells. It would be like trying to institute TQM in a manufacturing plant that had no defined production process and no specifications for the incoming material or the finished goods of each work-cell. However, by instituting a complete, detailed, and integrated marketing/sales process, the time-proven tool of quality management — among others — can be applied.

Note that the key to improving the contribution of any particular marketing/sales activity is contained in the basic understanding of marketing/sales as a process of linked activities. Thus, no "work-cell" within the total marketing/sales process (a System to Manufacture Customers) can be evaluated and improved without understanding what the upstream work-cells are providing and what the downstream definition of quality output from a work-cell should be. This basic tenet is at the heart of good manufacturing practice today. It can be successfully applied to Customer Manufacturing as well.

MARKETING AS A PROCESS

It can be argued that the sales function already has a number of available methods to order its activities into a systematic process. However, the concept of Customer Manufacturing takes these programs further, and, more importantly, orients the sales process to a whole new compass. We describe this in detail later, but briefly: In true Customer Manufacturing, the design of your sales process *starts* with your understanding of your customer's *buying* process. This buying process, in turn, is one of the things that is assessed in the Environmental Influences Assessment segment of the Customer Manufacturing process. Each and every element and step of your selling process is thus keyed off of a corresponding activity in your customer's buying process. By using a Customer Manufacturing construct you are forced to sell in the way that your customer wants to buy—not the way you might prefer to sell. (For more discussion of this topic, see Chapter 11.)

However, no one would seriously argue that the "front-end" of marketing has ever been a well-ordered process—let alone a well-ordered *and* effective one. One of the main benefits of the Customer Manufacturing construct is that it provides a coherent and complete process model for these front-end activities: Whether you use our specific constructs of Environmental Influences, Value Specification and Solution Development, or other equivalents, having a true process in place for these functions—particularly a process that integrates with sales and product development — is something that most companies have never experienced.

Employing a marketing/sales process model does not require the invention of any new marketing or sales techniques. A well-constructed process model uses common marketing, sales and corporate resources and general management skills, but it combines them in a new way. It defines a new *process*, a way to *integrate* existing or known activities so that they support and reinforce each other, and together compose a unified marketing/sales function that's integrated with other corporate functions and processes.

The concept of Customer Manufacturing defines marketing and sales both broadly and in detail. It therefore allows for clear job definitions and project goals, and exposes skills gaps. The use of such a structured model defines a common language, process, and format for marketing and sales activities across time, business units, and projects. It can ensure the completeness of the data used in decision-making, it forces appropriate data analysis, and it demands essential decisions. As a repeatable process, it promotes organizational learning and clearly establishes the role and value of marketing and sales.

INTEGRATED WITH PRODUCT DEVELOPMENT

One of the main requirements of any useful marketing/sales process is that it is explicitly designed to integrate with structured product development processes (or expanded, post-critical stage product development processes like Product Life-cycle Management) of the sort that most competitive companies have adopted. A structured marketing process is a necessary part of a structured Product Development process—without it, a Product Development process lacks direction and market feedback and, as discussed earlier, simply becomes a product development process at best. By design, the marketing decisions demanded at various points during a phase-review-type development process are the natural output of a correctly constructed marketing/sales process.

A useful marketing/sales process further defines the communication links between these two processes (marketing and product development), and the data that will be communicated at those decision points. It forces these communications to happen and to replace the time spent on ad-hoc, unstructured meetings, thus keeping the two organizations synchronized. It allows administrative communications (such as status reports and "over-the-wall" requirements) to be replaced by defined decision points with appropriate data available for those decisions. It defines the makeup and role of a Corporate Marketing Committee that is analogous to the Product Approval Committee defined in many structured product development processes. It also establishes links to projects' core teams and defines a high-leverage role for marketing management.

A STATE PROCESS

In a new product development context, the front-end marketing activities designed to support product development constitute a *state process* — in contrast to a linear process that proceeds from one step to another. A linear process review is concerned with the health of a process at a single point; a state process review is concerned with the health of all of the interacting elements within the process and with the health of the interactions themselves.

In a linear process, such as a phase-review type process, used in high performance product development efforts, once a process point, or phase, is passed, it is complete, and the process moves onto the next point, or phase.[38] By contrast, in a state process, all the elements are continuously active. For example, once a product specification is drawn up and agreed upon, it is not usually revisited.[39] However, market research, opportunity identification, and promotional tactics are continually ongoing activities and are continually revisited and tuned. (See Figure 4-2.)

38. It is true that there are many cyclic and iterative activities in any engineering or Product Development (as used here) process. Our point here is that an overall Product Development process moves (or should move) steadily forward. The whole point, after all, is to reach the end-point of a fully developed product. Marketing, by contrast, is much more state-like, in that it more-or-less continuously churns the same decisions, while outputting different information based on the continuously changing environment.

39. Both marketing and product development processes have various degrees of re-visiting activities. But the re-visiting of activities that a product development process does, such as in tweaking of the specification based on on-going market changes, or the changes to the specification based on engineering trade-offs, occurs at a lower level in a higher-level overall product development process, which is a linear process. Contrast this to the marketing process, in which all activities, information, and decisions are constantly being re-visited at the highest level of the process.

In a marketing/sales process based on the manufacturing analogy, a formal review process, in this case a state review process, relying on the measurements specified at each work-cell, replaces the ad-hoc marketing decision making that usually occurs in organizations. Ad-hoc[40] "non-processes" tend to generate "non-decisions" or reactionary decisions, resulting in wasted time and missed opportunities. Of course, such confusion and "un-management" greatly lowers morale and productivity, and the most talented people tend to leave such organizations.

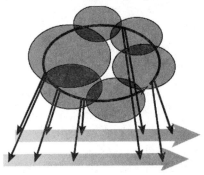

Marketing Process
- State Driven
- State Review Measured

Product Development Processes
- Phase Review Driven
- Phase Review Measured

Figure 4-2

The decisions to be made in these reviews are defined. The completeness of the data at each stage in the process is reviewed and the quality of the output of each work-cell is examined. State reviews, in a process driven environment, force the right level of management involvement at the right time, thus avoiding management "mines" — those gigantic problems that suddenly blow up on management with no warning. It also eliminates management involvement at too low a level, which is all too common and highly counter-productive.

MINIMUM NECESSARY SPECIFICATION

A useful marketing/sales process model is a *minimum necessary specification* of the marketing/sales process. It defines a marketing/sales process only to the extent necessary to ensure that all marketing activities are done completely and coordinated properly. It is flexible enough by design to be adaptable to business units and entire corporations of almost any size. And it accommodates the specific organizational and market characteristics of a particular situation. It does not straight-jacket an organization into rigid formality; rather, it guides it through a complete and thorough examination of the market, its opportunities, the de-

---

40. Note that we are using the term "ad-hoc" here with its usual, common meaning, which should not be confused with the technical meaning of an "ad-hoc" process described earlier.

velopment process and promotional tasks. It provides a structure upon which to build a company-specific process. As Geoffrey Moore once said, "A model's just a trellis. Your object is to grow a rose."[41]

FORWARD LOOKING

Any useful marketing/sales process model is forward looking. It is concerned with mapping present efforts to future states. By design, it avoids the fatal mistake of reacting to a competitor's or the market's present state — it forces decisions to be made on the basis of anticipated future states. High-technology companies in particular need to be acutely aware of the differences in marketing tactics and strategies during different time periods. In *Crossing the Chasm*, Geoffrey Moore points out that appropriate marketing activities, during the next product life stage, are often not just different, but the *opposite* of the appropriate marketing approach during the existing stage.[42]

In the last 50 years, we have witnessed the great strides that manufacturing has made as a result of becoming process-driven and managing that process with proven techniques. This same approach — applied to marketing/sales — will define the winners and losers in the early decades of the 21st Century.

41. "An Interview with Geoffrey Moore," Marketing Computers, (October, 1995), S10-S16.

42. Moore, (New York: HarperCollins, 1991)

5

C H A P T E R   F I V E

yes you can

In previous chapters, we have discussed the necessity of an overarching, comprehensive, detailed, information-flow process model of the marketing/sales function. In this chapter, we present an overview of the process model that we have used for several years now — the Customer Manufacturing System.

The Customer Manufacturing System is not academic theory—it comes from experience. It also has the distinction of being the only comprehensive process model of marketing to have been published (at least in part) in a leading journal.[43] It is a process model for marketing/sales. It is neither a straight-jacket nor a rigid set of rules. With such a process model of marketing/sales, measurement of and within the function can take place. And when activities are well defined and measurement systems are in place, true process improvement can occur—that is, marketing/sales can engage in continuous improvement — and other well-established process management methods can be employed.

Implementing a management structure based on the Customer Manufacturing System ensures both the completeness of the scope of marketing/sales activities and a way to measure the quality of each of them. It assures that the activities of marketing/sales are properly linked to other marketing/sales activities, as well as to appropriate activities in other functional areas.

43. Ralph Mroz, "The Synchronous Marketing Process," Industrial Marketing Management, May, 1998, 257-278

We view marketing/sales as an integrated set of four main elements, managed by three primary management principles. While each of these elements can stand alone as a part of the marketing/sales process, working synchronously can result in a dynamic, well-oiled production line in a successful Customer Manufacturing System. (See Figure 5.1.)

THE FOUR ELEMENTS

1. Environmental Influences are those factors that occur in the external world that you can monitor, analyze and predict—but not control. The factors monitored and analyzed include the usual market segmentation, market size and growth rates, customer demographics, and competitor information. Environmental Influences also goes further to address political, regulatory, and social influences, and those aspects of your own company that are beyond your control.

   The market intelligence you gather, through customer and competitive research, acts like a terrain map for your strategic decisions and competitive campaign. Most companies gather some of this data now, but few do so in a comprehensive and rigorous manner. This data can provide you with an invaluable advantage, if you have the systematic capability to collect, analyze, understand, and act on it.

2. Value Specification is the process of understanding and agreeing upon *Who* buys and *What* they are buying—or what they want to buy — from you that they can't buy from others. It's just that simple ... and just that tough. But many companies fail because they make assumptions about their customers, rather than ask questions from their customer's point of view.

   In a world full of smart competitors, it's your job to find customers you are uniquely qualified to serve — they are your Who. You must then determine exactly what these customers want, need, and expect to buy from you and no one else — this is your *What*.

   Value Specification — objectively determining your *Who* and *What* — provides some of the greatest leverage available to your company and its bottom line. It is here, on the Customer Manufacturing front-end, that management time can generate its greatest return. It is also here that most fail to be objective and truthful with themselves. One of the main

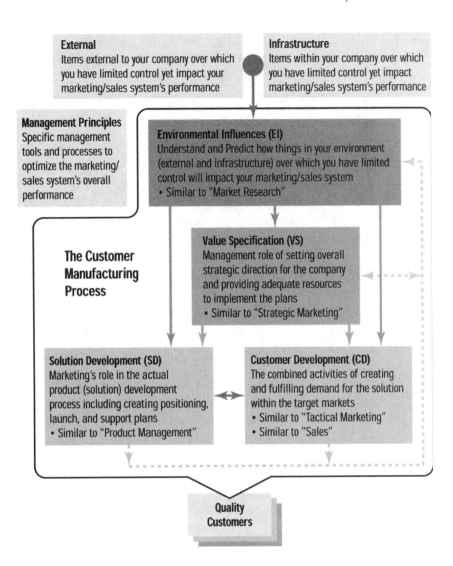

External
Items external to your company over which you have limited control yet impact your marketing/sales system's performance

Infrastructure
Items within your company over which you have limited control yet impact marketing/sales system's performance

Management Principles
Specific management tools and processes to optimize the marketing/sales system's overall performance

Environmental Influences (EI)
Understand and Predict how things in your environment (external and infrastructure) over which you have limited control will impact your marketing/sales system
• Similar to "Market Research"

The Customer Manufacturing Process

Value Specification (VS)
Management role of setting overall strategic direction for the company and providing adequate resources to implement the plans
• Similar to "Strategic Marketing"

Solution Development (SD)
Marketing's role in the actual product (solution) development process including creating positioning, launch, and support plans
• Similar to "Product Management"

Customer Development (CD)
The combined activities of creating and fulfilling demand for the solution within the target markets
• Similar to "Tactical Marketing"
• Similar to "Sales"

Quality Customers

Figure 5-1

elements of the Customer Manufacturing System is the notion of *explicit* value specification. That is, specifying your unique *Who* and *What*. Value specification is perhaps the highest leverage point in the entire Customer Manufacturing System. Certainly, it makes sense that the competitor that hits a hot market with the perfect product/service will have that market to lose … and that's usually what happens in truly competitive markets.

By spending time in the beginning — aiming before you fire — you will greatly increase your chances of hitting the mark. If you know exactly Who buys your product, you can reach them effectively. If you determine exactly What they (want to) buy from you, you can provide it to them.

3. Solution Development is the set of marketing activities focused on actually creating the complete solution you bring to market. Here, your marketing department works closely with your product development function throughout the product/service development cycle. The activities composing Solution Development are based on the market and customer intelligence gathered in Environmental Influences and the decisions made in Value Specification.

   Knowing the opportunities and constraints that Environmental Influences impose and understanding your *Who* and *What*, allows you to define product features, develop necessary customer support programs, identify the most opportune time for product launch, and determine appropriate pricing, terms and conditions.

   Just as design engineers and manufacturing engineers now work together in teams to successfully produce products, your marketing and product development teams must work in seamless synchronization during Solution Development to achieve the solution your customers want to buy. The Solution Development element is explicitly designed to work with the type of structured product development process that many effectively managed companies are now instituting.

4. Customer Development is the customer-facing side of marketing/sales. It consists of creating demand for your product and fulfilling that demand. Here, you set strategy for sales, promotion, channels and every other aspect of the company that touches the prospect or customer. You define all of the various audiences that you must reach and develop the right message for each of them. You design your selling process to accurately mirror your customer's buying process. And you implement these plans.

A critical aspect of Customer Development is the notion of aligning your selling process with your customer's buying process. In most companies, the sales process — the series of steps that the company goes through and the value provided to the prospect at each step — is designed to minimize the company's costs and cause as few headaches as possible. In other words, it is company-focused.

•• Samsung Nails Value Specification

Samsung is a case in point. Thought of throughout the 20th Century as a maker of cheap, me-too consumer products, the company now rocks in the 21st. As we write this, its televisions, cellular phones and other personal electronic devices are kicking butt in the market and winning design awards. Samsung is fast becoming the brand of choice among both hip and sophisticated users.

The company correctly understood the implications of consumer electronics becoming digital rather than analog. In this environment of accelerating and constantly changing technology, a focus on well-timed products can be a winning strategy, since there's little market left for latecomers. Launching a series of well-timed products requires impeccable value specification. To succeed, Samsung had to know explicitly what the market would want and precisely when – then not miss that window. This, of course, requires excellence in many operational disciplines such as product development and manufacturing; but without good value specification guiding the process, nothing else matters.

Value specification is a decision-making process that's all about having the right data and having the support to make the right decisions. New CEO, Yun Jong Yong, decreed that Samsung would focus on high-end products. He then streamlined the company to accommodate decision-making appropriate to the speed at which these markets moved. Today, using its native South Korea and its large technology-savvy population as a test market, Samsung can ferret out trends faster than its competition and refine the details of that understanding easily. By hiring more engineers and teaming them closely with market researchers, the company generates its own legion of high-tech product "probes" into the market and evaluates the results. Combining this technique of rapid prototyping with a close following of technology-adoption curves in its key geographic markets, it can come to market with a debugged product just as the window opens up.

Samsung rolls out new products every nine months, compared to twice as long, in some cases, for its competition. The strategy is working. The company is hitting its windows of opportunity. To do so, it must first define those windows. Samsung achieves this by orienting its processes around the key Value Specification questions: Who and What? ••

The problem is that the customer always has a specific or preferred process for buying a product/service like yours and they are more likely to do business with the company that comes closest to selling to them in that way. Customers have a definite set of activities they go through to buy. It is a unique sequence with a defined amount of time between the steps. At each step, they expect a specific "value" from your company. Trying to impose your timeline and your preferred steps on them, or providing them with too much or too little value at each step, will only cause more prospects to drop out of the buying process before they become your customers. This subject is explored in more detail in Chapter 11.

Figure 5-2 shows a comparison of the Customer Manufacturing functions as seen "traditionally" in a marketing/sales process, and from the viewpoint of the Customer Manufacturing process model.

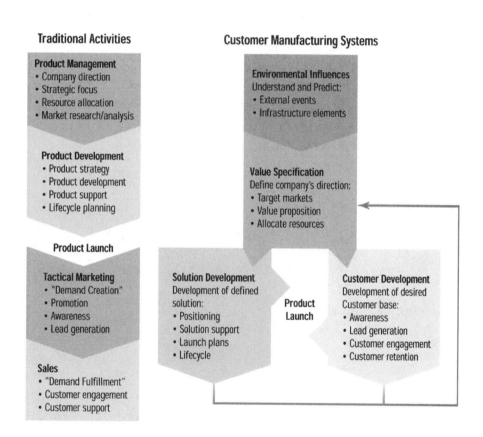

Figure 5-2

HOW TO MANAGE YOUR COMPANY FOR VALUE ACCELERATION

6

CHAPTER SIX

managing your customer manufacturing process

The effective management of marketing/sales is and has been elusive for most companies. Getting your arms around all of the issues necessary to understand what is going on in marketing/sales and how to improve performance is a continual challenge. It can be like trying to nail Jell-O® to the wall. That doesn't mitigate the need to manage the process; it just makes for a lot of excuses as to why it's not done well. Given the amount of effort that has been expended to find a useful, consistent management solution for marketing/sales, the question is: Is it really even possible?

We believe the answer is an unequivocal yes. The answer is available by recognizing that similar problems have confronted other business processes in the past and those problems were solved by identifying a set of management methods that could be used to improve results and provide a more manageable process. That is not to suggest that these prior problems were solved easily or that the first methods attempted worked. Rather, it was a long arduous task. Today's marketing/sales managers have the benefit of knowing which of those previously identified management principles worked and skipping the ones that didn't.

THE ANALOGY

One of the key reasons marketing/sales has been so difficult to manage is that it is an amorphous process in most people's minds. The definition of marketing varies depending on whether you are talking to an academic, a product marketing person, a marketing communications expert, a sales person, or a CEO.

This is further compounded by the fact that the way marketing links to sales is a mystery to most people. If we look at a process representation of marketing/sales, we find that Figure 6-1 represents a useful example.

Figure 6-1

This simple process representation shows marketing/sales as a process that starts with marketing and ends with sales, but which has a disconnect between marketing and sales. Most practitioners in the field of marketing or sales would concur that there is a definite disconnect between marketing and sales and that it occurs in different places within different companies, depending on how marketing/sales is organized. Trying to manage this process effectively and close the gap that exists between marketing and sales has been a dilemma for decades.

Examples of this disconnect can be seen in the real world all the time. How many times have you seen (or been victimized by) the situation where a customer shows the company's sales person an ad announcing a new product or service, a discount or a special purchase program, or some other event that is designed to have a major impact on sales revenue, only to find that the sales force has not been told about this event in advance? To be fair, we have seen a similar number of situations where, although the sales force had been told in advance, they missed the announcement.

Another example of a "black hole" disconnect between sales and marketing involves competitive intelligence. How often have you seen important competitor intelligence mentioned by a marketing professional at a marketing/sales conclave, only to have a field sales person casually remark, "Oh, yeah. We saw them doing that a few months ago...."?

In the late 1970s, when the Japanese semiconductor manufacturers were making their first moves into the random-access memory (RAM) market, they did so by cutting prices dramatically. "This reported action was ignored by most U.S. memory-product marketing managers at the time as the typical whining of a sales force looking for lower prices to offset their inability to sell. Unfortunately, for too many U.S. companies, this market intelligence was ignored to their own detriment.

One could ask how such important linkages could be broken time-after-time and not get fixed. But those of us who have worked in any company for any period of time — in either sales or marketing — know that this situation is all too common. Lack of process discipline is the root cause of the recurrence.

To solve this problem, it is helpful to find an analogous process for which solutions have been found. That analogous process is the design/production process, or the so-called "product manufacturing process." Let's consider an analogy. If you look at Figure 6-2, it is remarkably similar to Figure 6-1. Figure 6-2 represents the state of the design/production process about 30 years ago.

Figure 6-2

That is, 30 years ago, in most companies, the design/production process was a simple process that suffered from a disconnect between design and production. Again, where the disconnect occurred depended on whether it was the view-point of a practitioner — in either design or production — or an academic. The bottom line was, regardless of where the transition was supposed to occur, the gap was likely to exist. This gap — and the vagaries of the production "art" in many industries — caused a great deal of consternation on the part of management. It had a direct impact on their ability to forecast shipments, manage quality, or reliably predict manufacturing results. Sound familiar?

It is no secret that this problem has been solved in the design/production (product manufacturing) process over the last 30 years. Most manufacturing companies today, regardless of where they are based, use a combination of management methods to effectively manage the product manufacturing process. If a manufacturing company is incapable of using these methods today, they are likely to quickly become non-competitive in their market.

44. This price cutting method for new market entry by the Japanese, subsequently copied by other low-cost suppliers, is discussed further in It's Not Rocket Science: Using Marketing to Build a Sustainable Business, Mitchell Goozé, (Santa Clara: IMI 1997, 2002) 283-284, 289-291

Can these same management methods be successfully applied to improving the management of the marketing/sales process? Unequivocally, yes. If you look at the marketing/sales process as a Customer Manufacturing process — just as design/production is a product manufacturing process — the analogy is compelling.

BASIC ASSUMPTIONS

There are two basic assumptions that govern the applicability to marketing/sales of the proven management principles discussed below. The first assumption is that marketing/sales is indeed a process. While managed in most companies as a disconnected set of activities, which are loosely coupled at best, the reality is that the activities are supposed to create a process.

We've all heard marketing/sales described as a set of functional silos. This is too often true. Either out of ignorance or the desire to protect their jobs, too many marketing people perpetually execute functions that may never be connected to ultimately creating sales.

The second assumption that governs the applicability to marketing/sales of the proven management principles is that the process can be viewed as a "manufacturing" construct. If the desired output of the marketing/sales process is a predictable, steady and sufficient stream of loyal, profitable customers, then viewing the marketing/sales process as a manufacturing process to produce the desired output seems reasonable.

The steadiness and predictability of any manufacturing process is dependent on the existence of state-of-the-art management methods, as well as the influence of outside, possibly uncontrollable, factors. Neverthe-

•• Silos

One of our clients called us into a meeting to discuss the need to generate leads. They had a budget to generate leads and the lead generation team had been tasked and measured on their ability to generate leads. When we asked the purpose of generating leads, we received blank stares. These stares were the result of two different answers. The first was, "It is the job of the lead-generation team to generate leads. So, the purpose of generating leads is that it's our job." The second answer was a bit more useful (but only a bit, as it turned out). That answer was, "To help increase sales."

This, at least, seemed promising, so we asked where the leads went after they were generated. Again, more blank stares, until someone volunteered that they went to the lead qualification call center and probably to field sales after that. That too seemed promising, until we made a call to the lead-qualification call center to determine how many leads they could handle in what time

94

frame. The response was, "None for at least six-months. We're overloaded and can't get any more employees at this time."

After hearing this, we suggested that generating more leads in the short-term was probably not in the company's best interest. The manager of the lead generation group terminated our contract. (We believe the money they saved was used to generate more leads.) • •

less, as product manufacturing has evolved over the years, steadiness and predictability have increased. While we concede that outside factors in a Customer Manufacturing process may always be more influential than they are in a product manufacturing process, that does not mitigate the ability to improve the management and productivity of a Customer Manufacturing process. In truth, many of the objections to this analogy are identical to the objections that were voiced in the early days of the conversion of product manufacturing from an ad-hoc set of disconnected activities between design and production to the well-managed processes that exist today.

PROCESS MANAGEMENT PRINCIPLES

There are three time-proven process management principles that can be applied to marketing/sales. Those principles are: Constraint Analysis, Lean Thinking, and Continuous Improvement. We will review each of their meanings and describe their applicability to marketing/sales.

CONSTRAINT ANALYSIS

Constraint Analysis has been around for a long time as a mathematical construct. It gained favor in the late 1980s and early 1990s in the manufacturing world, due to the publication of the popular book, *The Goal*.[45] Constraint Analysis ensures that your resources are assigned to tasks where they can make the greatest contribution to improving the marketing/sales system's performance. All too often, resources are applied to non-critical constraints because of inertia, politics, or a plain lack of knowledge about where the largest constraint actually lies. (For a real-world example of this, read the sidebar story on the previous page about lead generation.)

45. Eliyahu Goldratt, (Great Barrington: North River Press, 1984).

Constraint Analysis is a natural outgrowth of process thinking. Since the goal in most marketing/sales processes is to maximize revenue, insufficient revenue is usually the "problem" that surfaces as needing fixing. Typically, either the sales force is then told to sell harder or more sales people are added. Often, lead generation—an upstream activity in the process — is assumed to be the problem and the marketing communications staff is flogged, thereafter, to generate more leads.

Constraint Analysis demands that you look at the entire process of marketing/sales to determine where the real limitation lies in your ability to produce sales. Perhaps it is the messages you are delivering. Perhaps the messages are being delivered to the wrong people. Without identifying the real reason sales are low — the main constraint in the process — you will only be spending resources on symptoms, with little result. Special considerations in applying constraint theory to marketing/sales systems are discussed in detail in the next chapter.

LEAN THINKING

Lean Thinking refers to techniques used to eliminate waste and non-value-added steps throughout your marketing/sales process. Lean Thinking is the action corollary to the truism: "Don't confuse activity with progress." Each step of your marketing/ sales process must be assessed to determine the activities that contribute to the effectiveness of your System to Manufacture Customers and to identify non-value-added

• • Motorola Goes Lean

In the 1970s, the Motorola Semi-conductor Group's fledgling MOS Integrated Circuit Division in Austin, TX was notoriously poor at shipping on time. The company instituted reporting mechanisms to track actual shipments to customer commitment. When the practice of unilaterally changing the customer commitments mid-stream was identified as a way to report apparent better performance, the reporting benchmark became actual shipment-versus-first-customer-commitment-date.

This improved the ability to identify problems for awhile, until production determined that the "solution" was to provide a highly-padded first commitment date. This made production look good, but upset customers and made the division potentially non-competitive against suppliers that either performed better or needed less padding.

The new general manager of the division, Al Stein, solved the problem with a very simple process measurement tool he had brought with him from Texas Instruments. He called it "linear shipments." The first chart he wanted to see in his monthly performance reviews was shipments-by-week (ultimately changed to shipments-by-day). What Stein was looking for was the linearity of the shipments. Did the division still have a tendency to ship 75% of its products in the last week of the month (or, worse, in the last 2 days)?

In a typical four-week month, Stein pushed for — and got — 25% of the total month's shipments shipped each week. This ultimately became a virtually linear, daily-shipment performance. A funny thing happened along the way. Delivery time decreased; shipment-to-first-customer-commitment increased; production's need to pad the initial delivery commitment disappeared; and Motorola became a leading supplier of MOS integrated circuits (at a profit).

Of course, when Stein then suggested that linear bookings (new orders received) were his next target, the marketing and sales people revolted — saying that, unless he was going to order the customers to buy when Motorola told them to, linear bookings were not possible.

Upon reflection this request may not be as outrageous as it initially appears. Many businesses (and certainly Motorola) have large numbers of customers. Eliminating seasonality from the equation (which will have whatever effect it has, as an uncontrollable Environmental Influence), the reality is that customers, left to their own desires, would likely order in a fairly linear fashion. Certainly some customers' systems may issue orders at the end of the month, but others could just as likely order in the beginning, or middle or... For orders to "clump" at the end of a period is actually "unnatural" and occurs because many marketing/sales processes are designed, for their own

steps, which are either irrelevant or actually slow down the system. (For example, is it possible that the process you use to provide quotes to your customers is actually slowing down their ability to buy?)

Further, you must have a seamless and integrated marketing/sales process that allows upstream activities to contribute to downstream results. For example, is your strategy aligned and linked with your new product/service definition, or have they evolved independently of each other and separately from your customers' needs, wants, and expectations? Have you developed "marketing/sales silos" where activity occurs for the sake of keeping people employed — with no real understanding of whether or how those activities link to downstream activities that could be used to create or keep a customer? Lean Thinking is the proven management discipline that helps you balance your resources and minimize and ultimately eliminate waste. Lean Thinking, as it is applied to marketing/sales, is discussed in more detail in Chapter 9.

CONTINUOUS IMPROVEMENT

Continuous Improvement is the on-going, pervasive and systematic methodology by which quality, at each step in the process, is specified; and by which out-of-spec and sub-optimal performance is removed from the system.

Using a potent combination of Constraint Analysis and Lean Thinking, sub-optimal performance is redefined for on-going Continuous Improvement. The techniques most commonly employed in Continuous Improvement are pattern analysis, quality control, and training.

These three powerful and proven management principles have been successfully applied to improve the product manufacturing process. By applying them to the Customer Manufacturing process, companies can gain a significant advantage in their ability to manage, control and improve their marketing/sales process. For too long now, marketing/sales has been viewed as something that cannot be managed as a process — but rather as a function where success depends solely on gifted individuals. While great people can add significant value, the perception that they

internal "logic," optimal performance is to generate non-linear orders from customers.

As many of us have learned over the years, sometimes orders coming at the end of the month (or quarter) are due less to what the customers really want as to what the suppliers have trained them to do, by offering period-ending discounts that savvy buyers simply wait (or negotiate) for. The application of a part of Lean Thinking is what Mr. Stein was advocating initially in manufacturing and then in marketing/sales — that is, let's get our non-value-adding procedures out of our own way. ••

are sufficient is only accurate so long as no useful methods for managing marketing/sales existed. That era is over. Talented people will always be valuable. (They are certainly still immensely valuable in product manufacturing processes.) However, they have proven to be insufficient to sustain a competitive advantage.

Every other business activity has discovered the value of process management. Marketing/Sales remains the last bastion of a failed belief in the complete power of individual talent.

7

C H A P T E R   S E V E N

bottlenecks to increased value acceleration

T he Theory of Constraints (ToC) and its management application, Constraint Analysis (CA), have been successfully applied to product manufacturing systems to increase throughput for more than twenty years. The fact that marketing/sales is really a Customer Manufacturing process — one surprisingly analogous to the product manufacturing process — suggests that the management principles that have been successfully applied to product manufacturing can also be successfully applied to Customer Manufacturing (marketing/sales). Indeed, CA is an extremely powerful tool for effectively managing marketing/sales.

However, there are differences between Customer Manufacturing and product manufacturing. Understanding where the similarities and differences lie is important to successfully applying proven management principles, such as CA, to each.

CONSTRAINT ANALYSIS—BASIC CONCEPTS

Let's take a look at Constraint Analysis (CA), using a very simple example. The driving concept of the ToC is very simple: *In order to increase the output of any process, you must first relieve the most constrained operation within it. Relieving any other constrained[46] operation does not affect output at all and only serves to build inventory.*

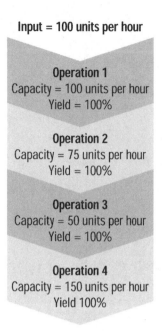

Input = 100 units per hour

Operation 1
Capacity = 100 units per hour
Yield = 100%

Operation 2
Capacity = 75 units per hour
Yield = 100%

Operation 3
Capacity = 50 units per hour
Yield = 100%

Operation 4
Capacity = 150 units per hour
Yield 100%

Output = 50 units per hour

Figure 7-1

As an example, suppose you have a manufacturing line that looks like Figure 7-1.

Here, obviously, the constraint — the operation that limits output — is Operation 3. Since every part must pass through Operation 3, the most the manufacturing line can produce is 50 units per hour. Working to improve the capacity of any other operation in the line will obviously have no effect whatsoever on the output of the process and will clearly just build up inventory within it.

So assume that you have now expanded Operation 3's capacity to match the system's input of 100 units per hour. Now the constraint on the system is Operation 2. At this point, working to improve any other operation other than Operation 2 will have no effect on the system's output. If you then improve Operation 2 so that it has a capacity of 100 units/hour, then you need to do further analysis. If the input to the system is constrained to its present 100 units per hour, then the best thing to do is to reduce the capacity of Operation 4 to 100 units per hour (which will presumably save costs). If, on the other hand, you increase the input

---

46. A constraint or bottleneck is defined as any point where demand exceeds capacity.

to, say, 150 units per hour, then you have three equal constraints — Operations 1, 2, and 3 — that need to be worked on in order for the system constraint(s) to be relieved. We'll see how this concept applies to marketing/sales further on.

Another useful concept from the ToC is that of *Line Balancing*. (Line Balancing may also be considered a component of Lean Thinking.) Line Balancing is often the first action taken in a manufacturing environment. In this case, it means to reduce the input to each operation in the line to the capacity of the constrained operation, so as to eliminate excess inventory build-up and excess capacity maintenance. In the example above, the first step that a manufacturing manager would have taken — prior to increasing the capacity of Operation 3 — would have been to immediately reduce the input to the system to 50 units/hour, as there would be no sense in inputting more into a system than it could process. (We'll also look at how this concept applies to marketing/sales later.)

The example above is simplistic. There are few manufacturing processes in the world that can be so easily modeled. Nonetheless, these CA principles — Line Balancing and relieving the main constraint first — can and have been successfully applied to manufacturing processes around the world. These processes differ from the example above only in the complexity of the process, but not in the CA principles employed in managing them.

MANUFACTURING PRODUCTS VS. MANUFACTURING CUSTOMERS

Successfully applying historically manufacturing-focused management principles to marketing/sales requires an understanding of the differences between the two types of systems (design/production vs. marketing/sales) as well as their similarities. While there are numerous areas where the two systems are similar, there are four significant differences between product manufacturing and marketing/sales (Customer Manufacturing) that can create problems if you try to blindly apply manufacturing-driven management principles such as CA to marketing/sales.

Both the product and Customer Manufacturing processes are complex and difficult. If you directly apply CA principles to the Customer Manufacturing process, you will simply map out your existing process, balance the process, and then go about relieving constraints in the order in which they constrain the system. If you try to do this, however, you will quickly run into some exasperating problems.

1. ***Defining desired output.*** The first problem you will run into is that the desired output of the process is defined differently. In a product manufacturing plant, the output required is whatever the plant is capable of producing, up to the level for which the company has demand for its products. Building more products in a manufacturing plant than the company has sold (beyond some minimum safety stock) is a waste of resources. A company's marketing/sales system — its System to Manufacture Customers (SMC) — does not usually have that limitation. That is, most of the time, a company desires more sales (output) from their SMC than they have.

   This may be to the company's short-term or terminal detriment. Several years ago, America On-Line (AOL) generated new customers at such a high rate that its infrastructure could not support it, leading to numerous and vocal complaints. Nevertheless, the company survived that episode and became, at least temporarily, the largest Internet service provider in the United States. Years before, there was the Osborne Computer debacle. Osborne announced a new product with such fanfare that customers decided to delay purchases of any Osborne products until this wondrous new product became available. Unfortunately for Osborne, their cash ran out before the new product was deliverable.

2. ***Dissimilar Inputs.*** Another area of difference is that, in a product manufacturing plant, a single activity may be fed by multiple, *dissimilar prior activities*; and the *dissimilar output* from each of those prior activities is necessary to complete the new activity (i.e., a door assembly may need a piece of trim, a door handle, the door itself, and a lock). The combination, or integrating activity, can run no faster than the slowest running up-stream activity, so balancing the other inputs to the level of the constrained up-stream activity makes sense.

   There isn't really an analogous situation in marketing/sales most of the time. (An exception could occur in a complex sale, where there was a shortage of field technical expertise requisite to support field sales people in closing their sales. In this case, adding field sales people would not increase sales. The capacity balancing required in this case is directly relevant to that required on a manufacturing floor.)

   What generally happens in marketing/sales is that there are *dissimilar* prior activities whose *similar, but not identical* outputs feed a common next activity. For example, there may be multiple advertising campaigns going on that all generate leads that then need to be qualified. This is akin to having three "identical" machines feeding to a common next machine in a product manufacturing plant. If the output of the three machines exceeds the capacity of the next machine, then either an increase in capacity of the "next" machine is required or a reduction in output from the three previous machines is indicated.

If this is not done, the work-in-process builds up in front of the now-constrained "next" machine. Output does not increase, but work-in-process inventory does. In a product manufacturing plant, deciding how to reduce the output from one or all of the three "up-stream" machines is straightforward because the output from each of the machines is known to be identical. Therefore, shutting one machine down, reducing the output from all three machines, or some other combination, changes neither the quality nor the kind of the input to the currently constrained "next" machine.

In marketing/sales, if the constrained activity can't be increased, then a reduction in output from the prior activities is also indicated. However, since these prior activities are different in function — with "similar" output, but of a different quality — an analysis needs to be done to determine which one to decrease. For example, the leads from three different advertising or promotion campaigns may not be identical in type and probably aren't identical in terms of "quality;" therefore, deciding how to reduce the output from these upstream activities is more difficult and requires a more in-depth analysis of their "quality" and cost.

3. ***Balancing with quality specification changes.*** In a manufacturing process, each operation has defined quantitative parameters that must be met. Should the output from a manufacturing operation not meet these parameters (e.g., the part is out of spec), then that output (the out-of-spec part, in this example) is waste and cannot be used by the downstream activity. That is, an operation either meets its quality spec or it doesn't.[47]

Further, in most modern manufacturing plants today, yield at almost all stages approaches 100%. When it doesn't, the state-of-the-art is such that spending money to increase yield is most often the obvious thing to do.

---

47. Rework may be possible; but in most modern manufacturing plants, it has been recognized that the elimination of the rework process is the objective.

Therefore, to increase the capacity of a typical, well-run manufacturing operation, you have to actually increase the processing capacity of that stage (e.g., add a shift or buy a bigger machine), or increase capacity (e.g., add another machine.) You would almost never "increase" the capacity of a production operation by lowering your quality specifications for the operation. That simply would cause the system output to be defective.[48] And you can't significantly increase an operation's capacity by increasing yield in the operation, since the yield is at nearly 100% to begin with. Thus, increasing or decreasing actual capacity is the course available to you.

However, it *is possible* to tweak the qualitative parameters (output specifications) in a marketing/sales system to balance capacity. Consider the following simple — but common — partial System to Manufacture Customers in Figure 7-2.

In a System to Manufacture Customers, you have another dimension available to you to work on to increase output and throughput that you do not have in a product manufacturing process. Not only can you increase capacity in any operation (by adding advertising or promotional campaigns, or by hiring more sales people for any sales step), you can also increase or decrease the yield at any step by changing your quality specification.

For example, let's assume you generate 50 leads at a trade show. If, for the purposes of this illustration, we define acceptable "quality" for a lead as "any lead from the trade show" (which is probably not a good definition but rather designed to illustrate the point), then the output from that trade show activity is 50 units. If, on the other hand, the definition or specification of acceptable "quality" for a trade show lead is changed to "only those leads who express a 'hot' interest on the show floor" (also probably not a good definition of "quality"), then the output from the trade show will be much lower—maybe only 5 leads. So, what is the output from the trade show? It depends on the definition or specification of "quality" for a lead.

---

48. Again, it can occur that too tight a spec has been set for a part and that the spec can be loosened, upon further evaluation, without affecting next stage or final yield. In well-run production systems, this is a routine analysis that is done to optimize the factory. This is different than what is described next for marketing/sales.

Figure 7-2

4. *Defining the time span.* In a product manufacturing process, the raw material input at the very beginning of the process is directly related to — actually a part of — the finished goods at the end of the process. Put another way, for any particular final output (finished goods), you can un-ambiguously identify and model the process that creates those goods. In a Customer Manufacturing process, though, in which we are concerned with the production of customers, it is not so simple, because you must specify the time span in which you are concerned with producing those customers. Are you concerned with next quarter's sales, or with achieving a market penetration over five years?

The most product manufacturing-like Customer Manufacturing system is one concerned with only short-term goals. Here, the definition of "marketing" can usually be shortened from its complete definition to simply "demand creation." This, along with sales closing, constitutes your Customer Manufacturing system. This is usually a relatively straightforward process to map for the application of Constraint Analysis.

Longer-term goals, however, are more difficult for two reasons. First, the process is itself vastly more complex. With longer-term goals, it includes not only promotion and sales, but all other aspects of marketing: research, analysis, strategy, positioning, decision-making, product development, and so on. Thus, it is vastly more difficult to map and to identify the input/output/yield relationships. Second, a lead can often be turned into a customer at various points in time and the trade-off between these competing courses of action must be understood.

For example, a computer manufacturer may decide to sell a prospect on a current model, and thus preclude additional sales for several years. Or it may decide to sell the prospect on a model that will be available in 18 months, and achieve a different projected lifetime revenue stream from that customer. Which course of action is the better one? That depends on the time-frame in which the Customer Manufacturing system is considered. And it should go without saying that the longer the time period involved and the less precise the data, the more qualitative the constraint analysis must be.

So, for these four reasons, applying the powerful tool of Constraint Analysis to Customer Manufacturing is a more difficult and specialized discipline than applying the same tools to product manufacturing. But if your process for marketing/sales is truly well defined — as it should be — the principles certainly do apply.

USE OF CONSTRAINT ANALYSIS TO INCREASE THROUGHPUT IN A SYSTEM TO MANUFACTURE CUSTOMERS

So how do you go about increasing output (sales) or throughput (the rate at which sales occur) in a marketing/sales system? You use the same tools that your manufacturing counterpart does, but you apply them a little differently.

DEFINE AND MAP THE PROCESS

You can do nothing until you understand your process. And you do have one. It may or may not be effective, efficient, or even rational, but you have one that's operating. You have to understand it and use common process mapping methods to capture it. According to the American Productivity and Quality Center, a process map is a picture of a business process or system sufficiently detailed to facilitate meaningful improvements.[49] According to the APQC, a process map reveals how an organization is structured, how work is accomplished, and what an individual or small group does within the process.

CONSTRAINT IDENTIFICATION

The next step is to identify where in the process is the major (top) constraint or bottleneck. As was described previously, adding capacity anywhere in the process — except at the point of the top constraint (bottleneck) — will not increase sales (output). For reasons also discussed previously, this can sometimes be a complex task in the marketing/sales process, either because constraints may have been created by artificial or arbitrary definitions of "quality," or because the time-span to be considered is non-trivial.

For example, how good does a lead have to be to move to the next step in the marketing/sales process? Do you have too few leads because of a lack of input? Or does the problem lie with your definition of a qualified lead? It may be either one or both. Further, do you know what ROI your new product has to generate to be acceptable? Is your lack of successful new products caused by poor research and market assessments made early in the process or by a product-launch process that is not working correctly? Because the definition of quality can affect capacity, it is more complex to identify the constraint in a marketing/sales process, especially if you don't have a good understanding of the process steps and what is going on up-stream and down-stream from each activity.

Nonetheless, identifying the constraint in a Customer Manufacturing process can be done to an acceptable and actionable level in almost all cases. And even if the identification does not follow a rigid mathematical formula, it will follow the beliefs and strategy of management. After all, the point of a Constraint Analysis is not to quantitatively enumerate the precise dollar loss that one constraint or another is causing—it is rather to rank the constraints so that you work on the top one first.

49. "APQC Process Mapping Course," Process Mapping Participant Guide (Houston: APQC, 2000), 2-4.

LINE BALANCING

In a product manufacturing environment, the first step prior to increasing throughput (the rate at which products are produced) is usually to "line balance." That is, once the constraint(s) have been identified, balancing the line so that the system runs at the capacity of the constrained activity is usually the best first step. Line balancing allows the plant manager in a product manufacturing environment to stop building excess inventory and to systematically increase output by relieving constraints in the proper order. This is especially valuable in a typical manufacturing environment where multiple sub-assemblies are used to create the final product.

Does line balancing make sense as the first step in a System to Manufacture Customers? That depends. One of the reasons for line balancing in a product manufacturing plant is to eliminate the work-in-process inventory that is making the plant less manageable and which may ultimately be unusable—and is certainly a waste of capital. Work-in-process in a System to Manufacture Customers can have the same effect, but not necessarily. Therefore, blindly focusing on traditional line balancing may not be the best approach.

For example, let's assume we have a tele-qualifying call center that is producing more "qualified" leads than there are sales people to handle those leads. Assuming that adding sales people to manage those leads would be profitable, but that the sales people are not available. This results in three alternative next steps:

1. Continue to process "qualified" leads via tele-qualifying that will become wasted; or,

2. Reduce the capacity of the call-center to balance with the follow-on sales activity capacity; or,

3. Increase the definition of "quality" of leads coming out of the call-center, so that the yield actually goes down for that activity (tele-qualifying). In addition to balancing both activities, this also causes the yield of the next activity to increase, and thus increase the apparent "capacity"[50] of the overall system.

50. This is a critical issue. As was discussed previously with trade show leads, the definition of a "qualified" lead from the call-center can be adjusted so that the probability of closing those leads, when passed on to sales, increases. If you increase the "quality" definition so that a higher percentage of those leads result in sales, you will miss some leads that could have been closed, even though their apparent "quality" was not as good. However, if you are currently constrained in your ability to follow-up on all the leads you have, one way to reduce the number of leads is to redefine what a qualified lead is before passing it on.

Therefore, in determining whether to or how to line balance in a marketing/sales system, it is critical to look at the effect on up-stream and down-stream yields, because "capacity" is highly "quality"-related in a System to Manufacture Customers — where that is not so in a typical product manufacturing system. Therefore, while line balancing may still be the best first step, how to balance the line can be materially different in Customer Manufacturing than in product manufacturing. Doing so effectively requires broad experience and a thorough systems analysis.

UP-STREAM/DOWN-STREAM ISSUES

Long ago (prior to 1984), and still today to a limited extent, non-local up-stream and down-stream issues, in a product manufacturing plant, were mistakenly ignored when identifying the cause and relief of constraints (especially at the points where production linked to design.) That is, assuming that the quality or throughput problems in production are purely production-related is a mistake that most well managed companies have come to recognize. Production problems may, in truth, have been "designed in" far up-stream by the design function.

In Customer Manufacturing Systems, non-local up-stream and down-stream issues within Sales as well as between Sales and Marketing and between Marketing and Product Development are critical to consider. As was briefly described above, in line balancing, it may be that the best approach to balancing a line may be to adjust (up or down) the definition of acceptable output quality of a prior activity.

Imagine that your company has a substantial number of potentially successful new product ideas that all exceed the ROI hurdle-rate necessary for acceptance. Assume further that you currently do not have enough engineers available to work on all of the new product ideas. (Let's say, for the sake of argument, that you do have sufficient resources to launch these products and support them, etc., in the marketplace, and that the true constraint is in getting more development engineers.) So, if you can't increase the development capacity by hiring more engineers, you will need to lower the input to the development function. The best way to do that is to change the definition of "quality" for the input. In other words, you can either increase the hurdle-rate necessary to qualify a project to be developed, or identify those products that will take less engineering time and select those first.

Recognizing the immense breadth and interplay of all of the up-stream elements in the system is a terribly important and complex issue in Customer Manufacturing. Because the "yields" at prior activities are highly variable, based on the definition of quality, and because the definition of quality can be adjusted, both activity and system "capacity" are especially fluid in a System to Manufacture Customers; therefore, making the correct decisions to improve throughput and output is complex.

WHAT TO DO FIRST

Based on the probability that management is primarily interested in increasing sales (output), instead of lowering the cost of selling, understanding the main system constraint is vital — otherwise the effort and resources spent are simply wasted.

The top constraint(s) can be within your system or a part of the environment. If the key constraint on the system is outside of the system itself (such as the lack of an available market), then increasing system yields is the only way to increase sales. In other words, if the constraint on your ability to sell more is the size or growth rate of the market, then you must increase your market share. To do that, you must increase the yield in your marketing/sales process, since a scrapped opportunity cannot easily be replaced. If lack of available market is not a constraint (and, often, it isn't), so that either your current market share is very low or the market growth rate is high, then yield is simply one way to adjust capacity.

Let's assume in the sales example in Figure 7-3 that the constraint has been correctly identified as being within the selling activities (as opposed to within front-end marketing activities). We must first consider line balancing, but the question is how to balance the line.

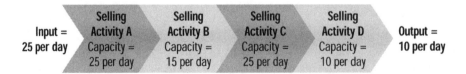

Figure 7-3

If the "yield" at each activity is close to 100% — as would be true in a typical product manufacturing system — then the obvious constraint-relieving solution is to immediately increase the capacity of Activities B and D to 25, since that is the potential capacity of the system at the present time. If that can't be accomplished "immediately" (and naturally, the term "immediately" must be defined and the trade-off involved in using that definition explored), then the next alternative is to increase the capacity of D to 15 and reduce the capacity of activities A and C to 15, as well as reducing the input to 15. If that can't be accomplished "immediately" either, then the sensible alternative is to lower the capacity at A, B, and C to 10 while also lowering the input to 10. At least in a typical product manufacturing system, that is the straightforward analysis.

But now, let's reconsider this situation from a marketing/sales perspective. In this case, the critical assumption that each operation's yield is close to 100% is not valid, so changing the definition of "quality" at each step can vary the output at that step as well as the yield of subsequent steps. In this case, output is still constrained by Activity D. In a manufacturing plant, we'd simply add capacity here. But in a Customer Manufacturing plant (a marketing/sales system), we have to identify the cause of the low 10-unit capacity.

Is it that the incoming "quality" is so poor that resources are being absorbed unproductively (analogous to poor quality raw materials in a manufacturing plant)? Or because perhaps the "workers" in this activity are being given good quality input, but are incapable of producing a better yield (analogous to poor quality machines in a manufacturing plant)? Or is some other reason at fault? Maybe even lack of enough people at this step (analogous to too little capacity in a manufacturing plant.) So it's not automatically a matter of adding capacity—it's a matter of identifying the cause of the inadequate capacity at the constrained operation, and fixing that problem.

Let's assume that we relieve the constraint at Activity D, and further we relieve the constraint at Activity B so that the system now has a through put of 25. The question is then how to further improve system throughput. At this point,

---

• • Time Horizons

We have conducted Constraint Analysis reviews for several companies using our computer-aided path analysis modeling tool. In every case, the top three constraints to sales (output) were identified using the concepts discussed in this chapter. For some companies, the constraints were heavily back-end loaded, making it easy to get short-term output increases. A very common constraint we have identified in several companies is either failing to recapture lost customers or losing too many customers.

we don't know if, for example, we should next lower the input volume and increase the yield of Activity A by lowering the definition of "quality," or perform some other adjustment. To further understand this issue and the possible solution set, let's look again at these activities, but assign names and yields to them from a typical group of selling activities (Figure 7-4).

In this system, we can process up to 10 orders per day, given how sales people work with the opportunities that come from the Evaluation step, assuming a 100% close rate (yield). However, the actual output is only 5. Why is that? Is the close rate low? Is the close rate high, but the time it takes to close lengthy? In the same light, what is causing the capacity at the Order step to only be 10? Should we increase that capacity by changing the definition of quality at the Evaluation step, should we add sales people to the Order step, or should we train the sales people to "close" more efficiently? There are many dimensions to the problem, and in the famous words of all consultants ... it depends.

Let's assume that the 50% yield (close rate) for the Order step is considered acceptable. Therefore, since the maximum output from the Evaluation activity that can be accepted by Order activity is 10, then the maximum output of the system is 5.

Oftentimes, the top constraint lies in the front-end of the process. Relieving this constraint (such as mis-identification of the correct product or service requirements demanded by the market) may not affect sales for many months. This can be frustrating to a company that needs to increase sales now.

In the manufacturing process, this is akin to the constraint of having products that are not designed for producibility. Redesigning the current products or fixing the problem in the next set of products to be introduced to production won't necessarily impact output tomorrow. In both of these cases — Customer Manufacturing constraints on the front end of marketing, rather than in sales or promotion, and Product Manufacturing constraints in the design activity, rather than in production — "back-end" constraints must be relieved to increase output sooner.

Probably the most intriguing "constraint" we have found among our clients was a fundamental disagreement about whether "output" was sufficient. In other words, were sales what they needed to be? Surprisingly, there was disagreement between functions on this "concrete" question. One of the top constraints in one company was the issue of infrastructure communications. It was pervasive. Until that was fixed, nothing else was able to function well. ••

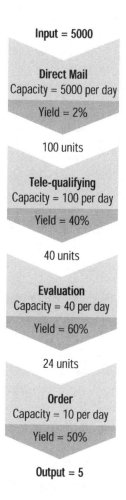

Figure 7-4

The capacity of the Evaluation step is 40, but what is the yield of that activity? Let's assume, as shown, that it is 60%. That provides a maximum output from the Evaluation step of 24, which exceeds the capacity of the Order activity. So running Evaluation at "full capacity" will generate more opportunities than the Order step can handle. To increase system output (sales) we can increase the capacity of the Order activity or decrease the yield of the Evaluation activity (because the assumption here is that increasing the "quality" of the output of the Evaluation step would increase the close rate at the Order step).

For example, let's assume that by lowering the yield of the Evaluation step to 25%, we can provide a "better" interested buyer to the Order step. If, by doing that, we increase the Order "close" rate to 60% from 50%, then the output of our system will increase to 6 units from 5 without adding costs (i.e., actually a lower cost per sale).

Alternatively, we could have added capacity to the Order step, so that its maximum input became 24. That would have required increasing capacity by 140%. This may or may not have been possible in a short time period. If it were, and if the cost of selling were acceptable, then this would have increased output to 12 from the current 5 at a similar cost per sale. Which choice is "better" depends on the situation and management goals.

This type of analysis needs to be done at each step in the system. It is thus easy to see why applying Constraint Analysis to marketing/sales is a job for experienced professionals working with senior management.

WHAT DOES ALL THIS MEAN FOR IMPROVING THE OUTPUT OF THE MARKETING/SALES PROCESS?

Management typically wants to assure both a steady stream of profitable customers over the long term and simultaneously increase sales in the short term. As Jack Welch said, "Anyone can manage long term and anyone can manage short term; it's managing both that's difficult." Therefore, the key issue in marketing/sales process management is determining what to do first based on available data. A useful analysis must, by definition, look at system-wide issues. That includes all marketing activities (including the front-end activities of segment selection, market research, marketing's interaction with product development, etc.) and sales activities, including those demand-creation activities that are often lumped under the over-arching term "marketing."

In virtually every case, there will be opportunities to gain short-term increases in throughput by attacking these sales activities, though they may not be the true constraint in the larger system. That is, there is likely to be enough "slop" in the selling activities (again, including the demand-creation activities often ascribed to marketing) that increases in sales can be realized in every case by working somewhere in the sales area, even though greater (long-term) benefit can actually be accrued by working in the marketing area first. But that doesn't always mean that you should work on the sales and demand creation activities first—it depends on management's goals.

Applying The Theory of Constraints to Customer Manufacturing (marketing/sales) works. Done correctly, it will increase sales and often lower the cost of selling. Like most management practices, it is hard work. However, if it were easy, there would be no competitive advantage gained from applying it, because everyone would have already done it. Applying Constraint Analysis correctly to your Customer Manufacturing process can and will give you a competitive advantage.

8

CHAPTER EIGHT

how to discover your bottleneck

As discussed in Chapter 7, finding the bottlenecks in your marketing/sales process requires the use of constraint analysis. Applying constraint analysis to a human system as complicated as marketing/sales can be done in a number of ways. Some are qualitative, some are quantitative, and some are combinations of the two.

Purely quantitative approaches can be implemented with relatively short time-frame sub-systems, in which the information that flows throughout the system can be represented with precision — for example, a lead processing operation. Qualitative approaches are in order when the time-frames are extended and/or the information can be measured with less precision, such as when evaluating the elements and results of a multi-year market penetration strategy.

Precision	Time Frame: Short	Time Frame: Long
Imprecise	Both	Qualitative
Precise	Quantitative	Both

Figure 8-1

But the fact remains that — regardless of the length of the time-frame under consideration, or the precision with which the data can be measured — the effectiveness of the process can be evaluated to a degree appropriate to the management of the process. Indeed, it must be, for the process to be managed at all, because you can't manage what you don't measure.

Just because an element of a process is not precisely, quantitatively measurable does not excuse management from measuring it as best it can, with the best tools available. If you aren't applying the most appropriate possible measurement to every element of your processes, you can bet your competitor is, and they will thus be better able to manage their processes — and obtain the superior results that accrue from superior process management.

The marketing/sales process model that we have described is an information-flow model. Information flows into the enterprise from sources, both internal and external. This information feeds a number of strategic, market, customer, and solution decisions, all of which are manifested in the form of information, which is conveyed to downstream, or more tactical, solution development, promotion and sales operations.[51] These operations then produce information, which feeds the downstream process elements, and produces feedback to the upstream elements.

So, to identify the constraint in the process, what needs to be measured in this information-flow process is both the information and its flow. The flow is relatively straightforward to measure: either downstream elements in the process are receiving all the information they need to do their job or they are not, and this can be adequately discovered by simply asking them if they are receiving the information flows that the process would expect them to be receiving.

To be certain that a complete process is in effect and to preclude ignorance of what is needed by an activity from biasing the feedback being provided by the downstream activities, you can also compare the expected downstream flows in the process being reviewed to a "perfect" process model that includes all of the flows that would normally be expected. The results of this inspection of the flows is a determination of whether all of the information specified by a complete process is in fact flowing, or if there are missing elements in the process. However, just because information is flowing (that is, being provided) does not mean that the information is sufficiently useful.

51. The terms "strategic" and "tactical" are hierarchical. That is, every operation of an enterprise takes direction (input) from other upstream or higher managerial level(s) and this direction becomes a portion of the strategy of that operation. That operation then develops tactics that support its strategy and produces information outputs, many of which contribute to the strategy of the downstream or next lower managerial operations.

•• Too Busy Gaining New Customers to Retain the Existing Ones

A major electronics products company was interested in learning where the constraints to sales were in advance of their sales meeting. Since a key purpose of their sales meeting (as with many sales meetings) was to work on ways to increase sales, they decided to implement a constraint analysis prior to the meeting so the focus of discussion at the meeting would be about how to do what was needed, rather than a "vote" about what to do.

The analysis was done using the methods described in this chapter. A key finding was that the sales portion of their marketing/sales process was executed well. That is, their ability to close new customers was done well. However, a glaring deficiency was found in their (lack of) focus on retaining and penetrating existing customers.

This is a common problem. Too much attention is paid to gaining new customers, to the detriment of existing customers. In this case, there was a strong likelihood that they were losing existing customers to the competition while they were working hard to attract replacements.

This, of course, results in inefficient and over costly marketing and sales investment. A decision was made to invest specific resources in retaining existing customers while

The information itself, as it applies to this marketing/sales model, has two relevant characteristics that need to be measured: its quality and its completeness. In other words, are the breadth and depth of the information transmitted sufficient, and is its quality, as measured by the downstream operation, acceptable? (In manufacturing terms, the downstream process element is the determiner of the quality of the upstream activity's output.)

If a marketing/sales process operation is receiving timely, complete, and accurate information from the operations that it depends upon, then (assuming it has proper resourcing) it has the tools it needs to do its job. Or in manufacturing terms, the operation's raw material meets spec. (The analogy to proper resourcing would be that the operation's machinery and people are working to spec and are of sufficient capability and capacity to handle the flow coming to them.)

Now, if all of the information flows, and the quality and completeness of the information that flows can be measured (to an appropriate degree) and you have a map of those flows, then you should be able to find the constraint(s) or bottleneck(s) in the marketing/sales process.

But, as we discussed earlier, in practice, determining the constraint in such a complex, human, mixed time-frame system is much more difficult than finding the constraint in a simpler, mechanized, uni-time-frame system such as a production process. (And not necessarily materially more difficult than finding the constraint in a complete design/production process.) To solve this complexity, you need a way to normalize (in the mathematical sense) the inconsistencies in the time-frames of the marketing/sales process elements and the differences in the degree of precision of the information.

also regaining lost customers. No additional marketing or sales investment was required, a refocus was sufficient. The results were increased sales, increased customer retention and the resulting increased profits. And, coincidentally, they suffered no loss in their ability to gain new customers. • •

Because of the information excluded from the results, such a normalization would necessitate further human analysis in order to extract the most relevant and actionable items. But it would still be a huge step in understanding what most constrains — and therefore what should receive priority in — your marketing/sales process.

You can do this by applying the fairly straightforward mechanism of asking an appropriate sample of relevant people at various management levels to tell you if every element in the marketing/sales process (including their own) provides the company with complete and quality information they need to do their job. When the appropriate analysis is done on this data, the result almost invariably pinpoints the major constraint to marketing/sales effectiveness—that is, the element in the process which is so under-performing that it is the major obstacle to overall performance. (Sometimes the constraint is actually a missing work-cell. That is, the process is actually not connected and elements assumed to exist are missing. In other words, you have an information-flow problem rather than a quality or completeness problem.)

In addition, such a data set reveals the degree to which the various organizations in the marketing/sales process (management, sales, enterprise management, product development, and so on) are aligned or misaligned. Sometimes such a misalignment can be the top constraint.

Using a causal modeling technique known as structural equation modeling (SEM) or pathway modeling combined with constraint theory, it is possible to obtain correct results from this approach using a widely-applied set of questions, even though the questions are asking for nothing more than opinions. SEM is a recognized method for converting qualitative information into quantitative information so that an analysis can be made and valid conclusions reached.

•• It's Not Just What You Ask, But Whom You Ask

Causal modeling methods are only as good as the model and method. Many companies we have interviewed have attempted to use a variation of this method (although not "scientifically") by asking a few questions of a small group of people.

Asking your sales people what the bottleneck or constraint to increased sales is in your company does not constitute a valid causal modeling method. It is simply a poll. To use structural equation modeling effectively, you must look at all of the work-cells in the process of interest. This includes gathering qualitative information from those work-cells, not simply the opinion of the sales people about all of the work-cells.

In truth, if you ask sales people where the constraint or bottleneck is in your marketing/sales process, we find the answer is invariably in only one of three areas:

1 Your prices are too high.

2 They need more leads.

3 They need more new products or services.

In our experience working with companies to identify the actual con-straint, this is rarely where the constraint actually lies.

So why doesn't everyone simply apply this methodology? Why doesn't management simply ask people in every activity in their marketing/sales process if they, and the people in every other activity in the process, have complete and quality information? In order to use this methodology, you have to ask the questions about a complete, integrated, overarching, detailed, and properly designed marketing/sales process relevant to the business under review. For the structural equation modeling method to work, you must have a valid model in place.

The reason most companies don't apply this methodology is that most companies do not have a truly complete, integrated, overarching, detailed, and effective marketing/sales process in operation today. The constraint in these companies' processes is likely a missing linkage or information flow in their process (that is, they have an incomplete or poorly designed process). Unless you know the complete set of activities and linkages about which to ask the information completeness and quality questions, you will not uncover the true constraint in your process.

Imagine an automobile manufacturing line that is turning out poor quality automobiles at the end of the production line. These cars are missing bumpers, air conditioning units, and even steering wheels. Yet a constraint analysis of the manufacturing line indicates that there are no real quality problems with any of the work cells, and they all have sufficient, good quality raw material to work with. The problem, obviously, is that this manufacturing line — the production process itself — is not properly constructed. It is incomplete. You can analyze it forever, looking for its bottleneck, and not find the actual problem.

Now imagine a marketing/sales process that is turning out insufficient sales, poor quality customers, or is otherwise not meeting expectations. You can analyze your marketing/sales process thoroughly and not find the real problem—the real constraint—unless you are comparing your process to a complete, integrated one. That's why you need a complete marketing/sales process model to use a structural equation modeling question set, as described above.

One tool that accomplishes this structural equation modeling approach is called Sales ThruPut Accelerator™ (www.salesthruputaccelerator.com). It applies an appropriate set of information completeness and quality questions in the context of a complete, integrated overarching, detailed marketing/sales process model — the Customer Manufacturing System described in this book — tailored to the appropriate market being served.

This computer-aided tool consists of a completeness and quality question about every element of the marketing/sales process for the type of business being analyzed, assuming it was as complete as the Customer Manufacturing System. The Sales ThruPut Accelerator looks at the entire enterprise marketing/sales system using a set of ques-

Structural equation modeling methods work, providing you have a useful model and you gather qualitative information about the entire process of interest from all of the people whose opinions are relevant. • •

• • Disconnected Activities Do Not Constitute a Useful Process

An industrial products and services company asked us to use Sales ThruPut Accelerator methods to help them identify the bottleneck to increased sales in their company. In their case the issue was that their process was comprised of a jigsaw puzzle of disconnected activities. For any given customer or prospective customer, a "process" was created to attempt to meet that customer's needs. This approach was rationalized by the perceived need to tailor the company's approach to meet the unique needs of each customer.

It is hard to argue with that desired outcome. It was straightforward, on analysis, to determine that not only was the goal not being achieved, but an opposite result was occurring in many situations.

Because each account manager had the "freedom" to attempt to create a tailored process to meet his or her customer's needs, in truth no repeatable process actually existed. It was impractical to determine if a complete process for any given customer existed, except to the extent that the customer complained, left, or was not captured to begin with.

Resistance to creating a useful process was rooted in the mistaken belief, discussed earlier, that process and bureaucracy are synonyms. Resistance to creating an adaptable process had caused the company to mistakenly believe that a disconnected set of activities was resulting in a useful process to meet customers' needs. The opposite was occurring all too often. • •

tions targeted to the top-level marketing/sales activities and top-level linkages in the Customer Manufacturing System.

If, on the other hand, you wish to analyze only a subset of the entire process using the same method, a specific set of activities within an entire marketing/sales process, such as promotion, product management, and so on, would receive a set of questions limited to that sub-system within the Customer Manufacturing System, and at a greater degree of granularity. And naturally, once a top-level constraint analysis has been done, a more granular analysis is usually performed within the sub-system(s) identified as the top constraint by the top-level analysis.

At least since 1985, with the publication of *The Goal* by Eliyahu Goldratt, constraint theory has proven a powerful and effective tool for identifying which management issue to work on first to achieve increased results. The ability to realistically apply this proven theory to marketing/sales has been itself constrained by the widespread inability to view marketing/ sales as a process and the consequent lack of sufficient data to understand what the system is actually doing. By applying simple, powerful and proven techniques such as causal modeling to marketing/sales, it is practical today to stop guessing what to do and increase sales.

Sales Thruput Accelerator™ v5.1r
"Sales Revenues"
Macro Assessment Questions v2.3

		How We *Actually* Perform This Today					How *Critical* This Is to Our Success				
		N / A	Strongly Disagree	Disagree	Agree	Strongly Agree	N / A	Not Important	Somewhat Important	Important	Critically Important
	value proposition, positioning, etc.) to accomplish its objectives										
13 Q	Its marketing/sales strategies are appropriate to accomplish its objectives				■					■	
14 C	The XYZ Company can identify all of the important changes that changes to its marketing strategies will require elsewhere in the company (organizations, staffing, competencies, etc.)				■						■
14 Q	Those changes that it identifies actually turn out to be necessary			■						■	
15 C	The XYZ Company can identify all the important changes that changes to its marketing strategies will require within marketing/sales			■						■	
15 Q	Those changes that it identifies actually turn out to be necessary				■					■	
16 C	The XYZ Company generates a complete set of goals (qualitative and quantitative) for each of its marketing strategies		■						■		
16 Q	Its goals accurately reflect what its strategies should accomplish			■					■		
17 C	The XYZ Company establishes specific marketing/sales resource budgets to support its goals				■					■	
17 Q	Its marketing/sales resource budgets are appropriate to accomplish its goals				■						■

Figure 8-2. *A representative output of the Sales ThruPut™ Accelerator*

9

C H A P T E R   N I N E

eliminating your wasted effort

L ean Thinking is a mindset that ensures the relentless elimination of waste throughout the process. What do we mean by waste? Waste is defined as any activity that is not necessary to add value from the customer's point of view. Lean Thinking, therefore, includes the evaluation of all processes, the elimination of processes which do not add value for the customer, and the modification of all remaining processes, so that each and every step in those processes add value for the customer.

The obvious benefit of the elimination of waste in any system is that waste adds costs without adding any value. Adding costs that don't add value translates into higher prices or lower profits. If you try to charge higher prices than a "lean" competitor, your customer will buy from the competitor, as they are able to get the same value for less money. If you reduce your price to match your "lean" competitor, your profits will be lower by the amount of waste in the system. Neither of these situations is good for your business.

As a concept, Lean Thinking seems straightforward and easy to implement; but, in reality, it is seldom practiced. Processes and activities within processes creep in to simplify the needs, wants, and demands of internal people, without regard for whether or not this actually helps (or, worse, hinders) the customer. It became popular in the late 1980s and 1990s to "rename" those internal people as internal "customers" in an attempt to justify these "suspect" activities as serving the "customer." However, this way of thinking makes it too easy to hide waste in a system.

We believe the adage: "You'd better be serving the customer or someone who is serving the customer" is wrongheaded. In truth, you'd better be serving the customer, period! If you cannot directly connect your activities and processes to adding value for the customer, then your activities and processes had better be mandated by a government regulation or it is likely that they are candidates for elimination. Simply assuming that, by serving someone you "hope" is serving the customer (or you call an internal customer) does not justify your efforts and often leads to waste.

Unlike with the Constraint Analysis discussion in the previous chapter, the application of Lean Thinking to Customer Manufacturing (marketing/sales) is virtually identical to its application in product manufacturing or any other functional discipline.[52]

THINK LIKE A CUSTOMER

The key to the application of Lean Thinking to Customer Manufacturing is to remember Rosabeth Moss Kanter's adage

52. For a more in-depth discussion of Lean Thinking, the reader is referred to Lean Thinking by James P. Womack and Daniel T. Jones (New York: Simon & Schuster, 1996).

•• Waste From the Customer's Viewpoint

Lean Thinking is one of the newest "manufacturing" management principles and has had very limited application to marketing/sales as yet. That being said, the first Lean Thinker was probably Henry Ford. His goal was to produce, every year, a car that was less expensive (but not less useful) than the previous year's model. He attempted to do this by relentlessly eliminating all costs that did not add value (in his perception) to the customer.

He vertically integrated his manufacturing processes because he did not feel others were as relentless at cost reduction by waste elimination as he was. (Contrast that to today's growing tendency to outsource non-differentiable processes to companies that can dedicate themselves to waste-free and, therefore, highly cost-effective execution of those processes.)

As a result of Ford's dedication to Lean Thinking, 50% of all cars produced and 50% of all cars on-the-road were Fords. Unfortunately for Mr. Ford, some of his beliefs about what added value from the customer's perspective were not true. He was in the habit of believing he understood how customers thought when, in fact, he appears to have believed they should simply think as he did. This weakness was probably most manifest in his famous statement that the customer could have a Ford in in any color they wanted — as long as it was black.

From Mr. Ford's perspective, color added no value. Changing colors cost production time (therefore, adding cost) and black was the most efficient color to use for a lot of reasons, including the fact that it dried faster. In the same time period, Alfred Sloan, at General Motors, realized that there were some costs the customer was more than willing to pay for. Understanding the important difference between a wasted cost and a value-added cost moved General Motors ahead of Ford in the market.. ••

to "think like a customer" [53] and avoid the often-substituted option of believing (hoping), as Ford did, that the customer thinks like you. The effective design of your actual System to Manufacture Customers — based on the discussions in Chapter 4 and Chapter 5 — therefore requires that the detailed process include only those activities which are necessary to add value from the customer's perspective.

Before you quickly assume that all of your activities are necessary to add value for the customer, start by considering your sales process alone. Is it designed to help your customers buy from you in the way (How) they want to buy, or is it set up to simplify your ability to "sell?" Regardless of the answer that comes quickly to mind right now, ask yourself this question again after reading the discussion in Chapter 11 about the application of Lean Thinking and customer-focused perspective to your sales process design. Once you have a marketing/sales process designed to match your customer's buying process, as discussed in that chapter, you can move to the next level of "Lean" and look at the application of the Lean concept of Kanban to the sales process.

KANBAN

Kanban is the Japanese practice that loosely translates as pull-versus-push by means of a signal-card (a Kanban). In a Lean Manufacturing system, the next work-cell in the process "pulls" from the immediately up-stream work-cell when it is ready. (The Kanban, or "signal-card," was the visual signal used in the original Japanese production lines to operate this "pull" process.) This is in contrast to the old (non-Lean) method of pushing work-in-process downstream as it is completed, thus creating potentially massive work-in-process inventory.

---

53. Rosabeth Moss Kanter, Rosabeth Moss Kanter on the Frontiers of Management, (Cambridge: HBS Press, 1997)

How does Kanban apply to the marketing/sales process? In numerous ways. Let's look at one in particular. The probability is that your lead generation is a batch-mode process. That is, you create leads in batches and pass them on in batches to the sales organization as you create them. The sales people then work on these leads when they can, which thus leads to one of two conditions: excess leads that are not followed up in a timely fashion (as defined by the customer) or lack of leads (or leads of practical quality) for the sales people to follow-up.

Which condition are you in? How do you know? Will it change "tomorrow?" In a non-Kanban managed system, there is no way to achieve any type of equilibrium in this process because it isn't measured effectively. Do you need more leads now, tomorrow, next week? Or do you need fewer? A Lean Analysis of your marketing/sales process is likely to uncover numerous opportunities to apply Kanban to your (and your customers') benefit.

ONE-PIECE FLOW

A related Lean technique is the concept of *one-piece flow* and it applies to the marketing/sales process just as much as to the product manufacturing process. One-piece flow describes the desire to take discrete items in a process and move them, as if they were in a continuous flow. The idea is to drive the moved item to its smallest "piece" (the so-called "one-piece") and to flow it, as if it were in a stream, rather than moving it in batches.

A bottle in a well-run bottling plant moves almost continuously. But manufactured items in non-"lean" plants move in batches that exist solely because of the belief that batches are more efficient. Individual items spend a long time sitting around, waiting to be processed; then, when the batch is complete, the batch moves. This is batch movement rather than one-piece flow. It has been demonstrated rather conclusively that one-piece flow is a more effective process than batch movement, which involves move/wait/move cycles.

Toyota was and is a leading proponent of Lean Thinking in their manufacturing processes (and elsewhere too). While U.S. manufacturers have stubbornly stuck to the belief that batch processing is more efficient and that "efficient batch size" is the holy grail, Toyota has worked relentlessly to make the efficient batch size as close to a one-piece flow as possible.

This relentless dedication has moved Toyota from an also-ran Japanese car company to a leading and highly profitable world-class automobile manufacturer. While other companies struggle to find Toyota's secret to success, it is out there for all to see. Toyota is a zealot at all aspects of Lean Thinking, including one-piece flow.

Two marketing/sales examples of a batch process involve market research and trade shows. Most companies do their market research in a batch mode. That is, they decide they need research, then they either commission it or have their in-house research department do the project themselves. This is a classic example of batch flow. Just crank up the research machine and go find out what we need to know.

To be fair, there are times when this approach is appropriate and can be considered a Kanban approach to market research. That is, the downstream activities have a need for specific knowledge, so they "pull" on the research department to provide the requisite research. This is certainly valid, but should not constitute the majority of research activity. The reality is that most companies have a continuing need for market intelligence. This information should be collected whenever and wherever available by anyone with access. This "one-piece" flow of data and information should be funneled to the research department, which can use it, as it becomes available, to make informed decisions to help the company succeed in the market. This research can then be made available on a continual basis, as required by decision makers.

Another example of one-piece flow is trade show leads. During and prior to the 1980s, the modus operandi at trade shows was to collect leads, batch them and bring them back to headquarters where they would be worked as a batch. This might include lead qualification, but often didn't because the incremental resources weren't available to process and qualify the leads. More often, literature was sent (overloading the fulfillment group temporarily) and then the leads were sent to the field for the hoped-for follow-up. When leads were received in a batch, the field sales person would have a tendency to review them, sort for the good ones and scrap the rest.

In the late 1980s, this batch process was improved by many companies by FedEx'ing leads back to the office daily. This reduced the level of overload on the fulfillment group. However, the leads were still usually batched for lead qualification or distribution. In the 1990s, many, if not most, trade shows adopted an electronic lead system so that booth visitors could be electronically captured rather than having to be recorded on paper. This eliminated the need for the entry of leads into a database. (A good example of removing a step which did not add value for the customer and which, in fact, probably injected data entry errors.) Today, most companies e-mail their lead batches nightly to headquarters for processing.

Why not take it one step "leaner" and transmit these electronic leads as they are received on the show floor? This migration to one-piece flow will improve the effectiveness of the fulfillment group. It may not help the lead qualification group since there is little that you can do to further qualify a tradeshow lead until the prospect returns, but the ability to see lead flow in real-time can help the company better staff its trade show booth and better plan for the qualification process to come.

FLEXIBLE WORK TEAMS

An important macro-process within Customer Manufacturing is the linkage between marketing and product development to create a truly multi-functional product development process. Whether you use a phase-review, a stage-gate approach, or some other method, you can create a truly effective product development function by including marketing in this process. However, to make it as efficient and effective as possible, Lean Thinking needs to be applied to make sure that the activities within the process add value from the customer's point of view.

A key element in Lean Thinking is the idea of flexible work teams (work-cells) as opposed to functional work teams. To keep the process flowing requires the ability to move resources where they are needed, as flexibly as possible. Without this flexibility, companies revert to batch processing so that they don't have to change equipment or set-ups as often. A truly effective Lean Manufacturing process requires the ability to reconstruct work-cells as required to deal with the flow as it happens.

Dealing with these demand changes and the ability to "flex" a work-cell is a requirement of effective Lean Manufacturing. This is equally true in the linkage between marketing and product development. Cross-functional work teams are mandatory for the process to work. The ability to create truly lean and flexible cross-functional teams makes the process work even better. For more details on this important process linkage between marketing and product development, see Chapter 12.

THE POWER OF LEAN THINKING

Of all of the management principles we suggest you "steal" from manufacturing to apply to marketing/sales, Lean Thinking is the most "immature." Its impact is just being felt by many manufacturing organizations because of its often counter-intuitive thought process. However, Toyota has been effectively using Lean Thinking for 50 years and credits it with both the huge transformation they have made in their company and the great strides they have made in re-inventing the automobile business. Applying Lean Thinking to marketing/sales can give you the same powerful advantage.

10
CHAPTER TEN

getting better every day

A JADED HISTORY

Continuous improvement is a concept that is often associated with the quality movement in the manufacturing arena. But it is really a much more far-reaching and universal management tool than that. It is, in fact, one of the fundamental management principles, period. It is so fundamental that to take it out of context — to reduce its context, really — and to look at it as *one of a number of things* that management does is to lose its relevance and to doom improvement efforts to almost certain failure.

Continuous improvement is not so much an activity, a movement, or a program— it is rather one of the essential foundations of survival that permeates everything that management does ... or should do. Isolating it to a particular functional area or in a specific program is a bastardization of the concept. Continuous improvement is a fundamental approach to management that is assumed to be present in all else that management does. Like reasoned thinking or pursuit of profit, it is so fundamental to management that it is part and parcel of its very core.

Continuous improvement took the form of the quality movement in the 1980s and dramatic improvements were made throughout the entire manufacturing world as a result. It is a rare manufacturing company these days — and, certainly, one on the short road to ruin — that does not turn out high-quality goods.

Seeing the spectacular results that the quality movement had produced in their manufacturing operations, too many CEOs fell under the misguided, self-serving spell of their quality consultants and instituted the same *manufacturing-based* quality programs company-wide. In fact, these quality consultants often sold management on the notion that unless *everyone* in the corporation went through their quality training program (taken from the manufacturing world), all would be for nothing!

Anyone outside the manufacturing function who suffered through one of these kindergarten-level charades rightfully acquired a very bitter aftertaste regarding the quality movement, and, unfortunately, regarding the overarching principle of continuous improvement, as well. Most deduced that quality — and by extension, continuous improvement — could simply not be applied to white collar work.

Nothing could be further from the truth. In fact, the best managed companies in history have always had continuous improvement at their core — throughout all aspects of the company.

Continuous improvement means nothing more than systematically doing better — because if you don't improve, your competitors will. It really doesn't get much more common sensical than that. Its most basic formulation is a five-step, cyclic process:

1. Determine what you want to accomplish;

2. Measure your current results;

3. Determine the constraints to performance;

4. Formulate a plan to improve;

5. Implement the plan/go back to step one.

Continuous improvement is a principle that applies at all levels of the corporation—from an individual's work to its outcome for the company as a whole and everything in between. Continuous improvement is not just a principle of management — it is a necessity for survival. Yet this basic management principle of continuous improvement has seldom been applied to marketing/sales.

SAME PRINCIPLE/ DIFFERENT APPLICATION

Several predictable reasons are offered to explain why continuous improvement can't be applied to marketing/sales.

- "You just can't measure what we do like you can measure tolerances on a machined part."

- "You can't assign quality measures to creative work or human interactions."

- "Continuous improvement is great for batch mode or manufacturing-line work, where things are done over-and-over. But what we do is different each time."

- "We work in time horizons of years, not days—how can you measure things that are constantly changing before they are finished? Besides, the people involved change too often to make quality management applicable."

None of these invalidate the need for continuous improvement. But the main reason they are raised — the reason they have been true in the past — can be found in a word so often used in these complaints: *measure*. The belief that marketing/sales cannot be measured in any meaningful way is the underlying roadblock to continuously improving the performance of marketing/sales. Most believe that any of the other four steps of continuous improvement are possible in marketing/sales; but few think that *measurement* is possible.

What's absolutely true is this: You can't manage what you can't measure. It is not so much that measuring the long-term, inherently changing, abstract mind-work — which comprises much of marketing/sales — is difficult, but that it requires intelligence, commitment and creativity. The problem is further compounded by the fact that, even if you measure marketing/sales activities, you still may not succeed in improving the performance, because the constraint may be upstream. You must make a commitment to true, system-wide continuous improvement measurement and management efforts for overall performance to improve.

When we look more closely at the objections mentioned above, we see that they are all really variations of the first: "You just can't measure what we do like you can measure tolerances on a machined part." Sure you can. What do you do?

Make sales? Perform market research? Provide field technical support? Set strategic direction? The effectiveness of all of these efforts can be measured. We have been measuring sales people for thousands of years — albeit often with the wrong measures (see Chapter 11 on sales process); but, at least, we have been measuring their results. Market research can easily be evaluated as to its accuracy, depth, usefulness, or any other measure we choose. Technical support can be evaluated as to its effectiveness (sale made, machine fixed, or whatever.) Strategic direction is reasonably simple to evaluate — with certainty after the results are in and with increasing certainty prior to that.

The key differences in measuring *marketing/sales* versus measuring *machined parts* in a manufacturing plant fall into these three areas:

- **The goals are different.** Determining what you want to accomplish in marketing seems more difficult. The quality spec for a machined part on a manufacturing line is easy to identify. Yet, the first step in measuring marketing/sales is also to identify which specifications and tolerances are important. The process begins with questions like these: What constitutes good customer service? What constitutes good market research? What constitutes a good strategy? Actually, once you ask these questions, their answers seem obvious. We evaluate people every day in these fields. Although we don't measure customer service by thousandths of an inch, we do measure it by customer surveys, management follow-up, complaints received and so on. We measure market research by its completeness, its usefulness, its accuracy, etc. We measure a strategy by whether it's getting the results we expected.

- **The time frames are different.** Manufacturing plants typically produce many identical parts in a day. Customer service may stretch over months; a strategy may be implemented over years. These extended time frames hardly make it impossible to measure results. But they make it imperative that management have the discipline to continue to measure results and to feed back the lessons learned into the next cycle. Since the players — including management — will probably change over these long cycles, the process requires discipline, not only on the part of individual managers, but on the part of the institution itself. This level of discipline and organizational learning must ultimately come from top management.

- **The measurements are different.** Instead of measuring hard, quantitative things — like mechanical tolerances of instruments — marketing/sales requires more qualitative measures. There's nothing at all wrong with that — use the best measure you have. Because the measurement can't be 100% "hard" does not in any way excuse you from measuring your area of responsibility as best you can.

STEP-BY-STEP

Let's review the five basic steps involved in continuous improvement:

1. Determine what you want to accomplish;

2. Measure your results;

3. Determine the constraints to performance;

4. Formulate a plan to improve;

5. Implement the plan/go back to step one.

1. Determine what you want to accomplish. No matter what your level within the organization—whether you are responsible for the output of a single individual or an entire company's marketing/sales — you must specify what you want your area or responsibility (your "work-cell" in manufacturing terms) to accomplish. (And keep in mind that you might have multiple goals.) This should be pretty simple. These are your objectives, which, in well-managed companies, have been agreed upon explicitly with management. Since objectives are, by their nature, measurable, this step should already be done.

One key agreement that needs to be obtained is the definition of output you must provide to the next downstream activity in marketing/sales. A key lesson management learned from manufacturing was that the only valid measurer of output from a work-cell was the next downstream work-cell which had to use that output. Marketing/Sales activities should not be done in a vacuum; therefore, the output of your activity can be specified by the downstream activity you are feeding. (This exercise is an eye-opener to many companies when they discover the number of activities for which there is no downstream activity. These activities have "sprung to life" over time and they now exist to keep people busy, rather than to increase sales. Review the Lean Thinking constructs from the previous chapter.)

2. Measure your results. As per the discussion above, there's always some way to measure your performance. (You know the downstream work-cell has an opinion.) What you need to do is to make sure that your performance measures actually correspond to your objectives. There are all too many organizations that are measured on parameters that have nothing to do with the goals of the organization. You need to ensure that not only are the performance measures used the best ones available or feasible, but that they have been agreed upon by the downstream activity. Finally, the hard part is to institute a rigorous measurement system and live by it day-by-day (or with whatever periodicity is appropriate for your task).

If you are a sales manager, you will probably want to track movement through the buying process (not your selling process — again, see Chapter 11 on selling process). If you are responsible for setting marketing or product strategy, you will probably need to track the alignment of that strategy with ever-changing market realities as the strategy is implemented. The hard part is actually doing it! As odd as it seems, *few companies have the discipline to continuously measure their performance.*

3. Determine the constraints to performance. Once you know what you are supposed to accomplish and how you are actually performing, then, if you are not performing "within spec," you will need to determine the reason why.

In the manufacturing world, *fishbone charts* have become a popular tool for visualizing the inter-relationship of the multitude of causes and effects in relation to performance. Fishbone charts are a simple form of constraint analysis and can be used if the cause of under-performance isn't obvious. The goal is to determine what needs to change (and how) so that performance gets back on track. This is seldom difficult, but it does require discipline and the ability not to get side-tracked by non-vital issues.

4. Formulate a plan to improve. Once you've determined the cause of under-performance, then it's usually — though, not always — a short path to figuring out what to do to correct it. The corrective action itself can, of course, be easy or extremely difficult, simple or very complex in nature—but do it you must. As Dr. Edward de Bono has wryly—and correctly— pointed out: "Knowledge does not always lead to action."[54]

---

54. Six Action Shoes (New York: HarperBusiness, 1991), 64.

5. *Implement the plan.* Actually doing something is the most difficult thing in the world. Planning, talking and documenting are easy. There are legions of companies with solid, well-documented plans on the shelf. Actually implementing them, for some reason, is where almost all of the shortfall is. It keeps coming back to discipline. If you look at the best performing companies of all time, it's striking that, although some of their goals and methods were pedestrian and obvious, the company was exceptionally disciplined in reaching them. To quote the famous Jedi Knight, Yoda, "Do or don't do. There is no try."

WHY A PROCESS MODEL IS NECESSARY

If we look again at the three main ways — goals, time frames and measurements — in which continuous improvement differs in marketing/sales from continuous improvement in manufacturing, we can see why an integrated, comprehensive process model of marketing/sales is essential. A process model — the representation of the process you are working with — is essential in any continuous improvement effort.

In the manufacturing world, it appears to be pretty easy to see what the process model is — the manufacturing portion of the process is represented in concrete form by the manufacturing line. (Of course, what people learned after many years of struggle in trying to improve the process was that an integrated process model that includes the design function is necessary.) With marketing/sales, the process model is more difficult to apply because we have to use paper diagrams and abstract representation. And it's the lack of such an accurate, overarching and detailed process model that includes marketing *and* sales that has been holding back the use of continuous improvement in the marketing/sales arena.

But by using such a model — one that details each work-cell in the marketing/sales function, one that specifies the input and output of each work-cell, and one that does all this at various hierarchical levels — we can overcome the barriers to continuous improvement in marketing/sales. We can specify the goal and its "quality spec" for any activity or group of activities in marketing/sales. We can identify the upstream inputs to any work cell and measure their quality. We can track measurements over long periods of time, because they're all down on paper.

If we understand the process, applying continuous improvement is easy; if we don't, it's impossible.

PART *4* FOUR

PUTTING THE PIECES TOGETHER

11

CHAPTER ELEVEN

breakthrough thinking
in sales

There have been countless books written on improving sales and billions of dollars spent on sales training. Yet, by all anecdotal accounts, the productivity of the average salesperson (adjusted for inflation) hasn't materially changed in over 50 years. That being the case, one of the positive trends in recent years has been the orientation toward true process thinking among leaders in the field. Another positive trend has been to view the sales process from the point of view of the customer, rather than from the internal point of view of the firm.

Even among those products (or services) for which there's actually a market, most sales efforts fail today for one of two reasons:

- The sales activities are just that—a set of activities, rather than a true process.

- The wrong sales process is applied.

A set of sales activities not organized into a process is nothing more than a chaotic, random group of events. The inevitable outcome — surprise! — is a chaotic, random group of results. Without a true process in place, there is no way to implement fundamental management tools that are required in any function, such as:

143

- Measurement and management

- Process improvement

- Reporting, coordination and pre-diction.

The only way to "manage" or "improve" a sales function that is not process-driven is to swap out sales people and hope for better results. Sound familiar? That's the way many sales organizations are run.

More sophisticated sales organizations today, however, claim to have a process in place. This may be true to some extent, but the process they have in place is almost always the wrong process. This is because most sales processes have one of two origins:

- They have evolved over time to be "efficient" in terms of dollars spent and internal work flow.

- They have been modeled after one of the popular sales programs sold in books or by consulting firms.

The problem with these approaches should be apparent. Sales processes constructed for internal efficiencies do little to make it easier for your customers to buy (which is one reason that re-engineering efforts comprising sales processes often failed.) And sales processes mirroring an abstract one-size-fits-all approach are unlikely to have relevancy to your customers.

•• A Transaction Orientation

One of our clients had developed a very efficient inside sales organization to support their transaction-oriented customer base. That is, virtually all of their business, in the early days, was from customers who bought once, and did not buy again on any predictable basis. Therefore, for efficiency reasons, they had developed a transaction-oriented sales mentality and process.

Their sales process consisted of inside sales people who answered the phone and served the customer. They did this very well and their business grew. However, over the years, the customer-base in this industry became more oriented toward what is commonly referred to as "relationship" or "consultative" selling. That is, many of these customers were making larger purchases more frequently and began to value applications expertise and proactive service.

Since the sales process designed and in use by our client was reactive and transaction oriented, their sales began to drop. In fact, their sales dropped during a boom in the industry. They had the right products, the right prices, the right service, the right expertise … and the wrong sales process to support their customers' desired buying process. During one of the greatest booms in their industry, their business actually dropped by over

50%, simply due to using the wrong sales process.

We know this because, by redesigning their sales process to be in alignment with their customers' buying process, we were able to stop the sales slide and increase sales, during an industry downturn. ••

Most organizations — from retail stores to large industrial corporations — have lost sight of the very purpose of sales: to make it easy for customers to buy from *you*. (Causing them to initially desire or be aware of your product is the job of promotion—not sales.)

The key fact is that *your customers have a distinct buying process that they go through.* They perform a distinct set of buying actions at specific times (or during specific time periods) throughout their process. Further, at each buying step in their process, they require value of some kind from you—such as, information (a brochure, pricing, specifications, deliveries, etc.); a visit; a demonstration; or simply being left alone. The buying activities of your customer and the timeline along which they lie are depicted by the lower line in the diagrams in Figure 11-1. The shapes represent the different buying steps; the distance between them represents time. The value they expect from you at each of their buying steps is depicted by the arrow going upward.

Figure 11-1

As you'll notice, the upper line in the diagram represents a typical sales process. Note that the steps it performs are not mirror images of the buying steps that the customer goes through. Nor are the selling activities synchronized with the customer's buying activities. The sales process starts and ends at different times from the customer's buying process; the one sales step that is a reflection of a customer's buying step is performed at a different time than the customer's; the value delivered to the customer at each selling step is not the value expected by the customer.

If you have ever bought a car — or a multi-million dollar industrial system — you will immediately recognize the dissonance we are describing between the buying process that you wanted to use and the selling process that was imposed on you. (This misalignment between the sales process and the buying process is the main reason that so many CRM implementations have failed—they have simply automated a bad process.)

Now look at the diagram in Figure 11-2. This is how a sales process should look: aligned with the customer's buying process. Every customer buying activity is mirrored at the appropriate time by a selling activity. The value expected by the customer at each step of their buying process is provided at that time by the selling process.

Figure 11-2

What are some examples of alignment versus misalignment? Two common ones are quotes/proposals and "end-of-the-period" purchase incentives. Let's look at quotes/proposals first. There are two different ways that quotes and proposals are misaligned with the customer's buying process.

It is not uncommon to find customers waiting for their vendors to provide a quote or proposal. Conversely, it is not unusual for a sales person to offer a quote or proposal to a customer who is not ready to receive one.

In the former case, the customer is waiting to buy, but cannot buy because the vendor has not provided a timely quote. What does this say (in the customer's mind) about the vendor's ability to serve the customer? While it may be true that the customer waited until the last minute to request the quote and caused the difficulty, we are reminded of the old expression "lack of planning on the customer's part does constitute an emergency on your part."

In the latter case, the sales person is confusing motion with progress by offering to provide a quote. It is quite simple for the customer to say, "go ahead," since the vendor has offered to do work without compensation. If you provide a quote before the customer is ready to receive it, you may quote on the wrong solution and you may be unduly burdening your quoting department so that they cannot be timely on quotes that do matter.

End-of-the-period purchase incentives are another common misalignment. How many times have you pushed your sales force to get orders prior to period-end to meet your numbers? We understand the real-world imperative of this charade, but the cost of getting customers to buy before they are ready in terms of price reductions or other incentives is quite large. Further, you are training your customers to expect an incentive. As we write this, the U.S. automobile industry has been running "incentives" for so long, that most customers won't buy a car without one any more.

You can avoid these problems and create a more manageable sales process by focusing on aligning what your sales process does with what the customer needs in order to buy. The throughputs and fallouts from one step in the sales process to the next can reflect what is actually happening in the customer's purchasing process, and predictions made about future sales events will have a relationship to some real event in the customer's process. In this way, process improvement — sales productivity — is actually possible, because the "quality spec" of each activity in the sales process is known: it is the alignment of that activity with the appropriate customer buying activity.

How do you construct such a selling process? Here are the steps you need to go through to do so:

1. Map your customer's buying process.

There is no Step 2. You've just designed your sales process. Now you can stop selling and start making customers.

12

CHAPTER TWELVE

getting products/services to market... successfully

M ost well-managed companies today employ some form of a structured New Product Development process (NPD), such as the popular phase-review and stage-gate processes (Figure 12-1).

Yet the GIGO (garbage in/garbage out) phenomena is still pervasive. These world-class NPD processes are still too often turning out products that are either unwanted, mis-timed, or off the mark. Why? Because the processes' basic input about what to make for whom — when — is faulty. Specifying these three things is, of course, really just a shorthand way of summing up the job of the front-end of marketing. Marketing is the weak link in NPD. Today, very well-managed companies are implementing an expanded version of a structured new product development process in the form of product lifecycle management (PLM). Although PLM by its nature is more integrated with marketing than first-generation NPD, it is still not fully integrated in the sense we mean. For simplicity in this book, we use the earlier term "NPD" to mean both NPD and PLM.

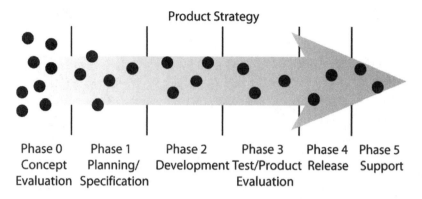

Figure 12-1

A review of the product development literature today reveals that concern with this "weak link" (marketing's effectiveness) is a dominant theme — one causing great concern. Study after study performed, sponsored, or reported by the Product Development Management Association[55] confirms that too little marketing involvement is a predictor of new product failure. In fact, many of these studies indicate the higher the ratio of marketing resources to engineering resources in an NPD project, the higher the chances of success. In some industries, best practices are that marketing personnel out-number engineering personnel by a considerable margin.

Processes that link marketing and product development are usually best keyed off of the structured product development process in use at a company. Any such valid process has some kind of stage or phase structure and filtering mechanisms for a project to proceed from one phase to an-

55. These studies are too numerous to list. See, the PDMA's website (www.pdma.org) for information.

•• IBM and the Fuzzy Front End

IBM Corporation is a company that instituted a structured product development process in the 90s. As a result, IBM saw dramatic decreases in product development cycle time and overall increases by any measure of product development effectiveness. Now IBM is doing something that pushes the envelope of the product development/marketing union even further.

The hardest part of any robust new product development process is what is called the "fuzzy front end" — that is, the ideation of new-to-the-world ideas. Traditional market research reaches its limits here — how do people tell you that something would be valuable to them if they have never conceived of anything like it?

IBM has found a powerful tool on the fuzzy front end. They now actively create partnerships for their research labs — not their development groups, but their way-out-there research labs. A researcher with a promising idea is partnered with business development professionals. Together, they work with leading-edge customers to attack their thorniest problems and test the potential of new ideas. The plan is to get real-world customer feedback about product ideas, as the labs come up with them, and thereby refine both the research direction and the subsequent product development for the ideas that have market potential.

This new approach is suited to both the new services focus of IBM and the fact that most information technology, high-value problems today are not problems that depend on advances in basic material science, but rather on service and software advances. Thus, customer-solution breakthroughs are not bound by the laws of physics, but by the focus of the research organization. IBM has tapped one of its greatest resources — its research brainpower — and found a way to accelerate its profit impact by folding it into the marketing process on the fuzzy front end of product development. ••

other. Clearly spelled out in these of processes is a detailed list marketing responsibilities at each phase from a product development perspective. A well-designed marketing process that dovetails with such a well-defined product development process enables the marketing deliverables at each phase to be complete and accurate, and defines the broader marketing process that makes that effective marketing/product development link possible.

As you'll recall, marketing is a continuous state process — one that's constantly reviewing and renewing its activities. This is only common sense — data and decisions must naturally be constantly revisited. Product development, on the other hand, is a forward-moving process. Indeed, one of the characteristics of effective NPD processes is that decisions get made crisply and on time, and that projects either move forward or die (or, in rare cases, go back to a previous step). These two processes — the functional marketing process and the multi-functional product development process — are integrated in the following manner:

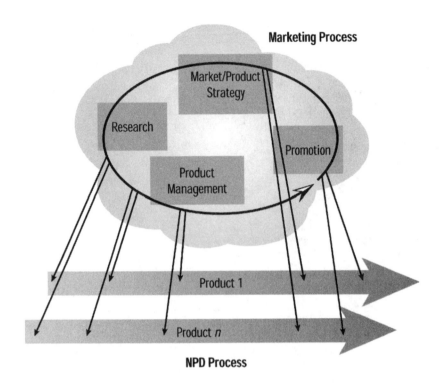

Figure 12-2

We see from Figure 12-2 that data and decisions from the constantly cycling marketing process are fed into the NPD process at the appropriate time (or phase, in a phase-review process). The trick to making this integration work — assuming that you have a robust NPD process in place — is to have a similarly robust marketing process operational, and to define the information links effectively.

In a preceding chapter, we have described what composes a similarly robust marketing process and have offered an example. Figure 12-3 depicts a simple example of the information links between this marketing process and an NPD process for two phases in a phase-review process.

It should be obvious that both a well-defined and complete marketing process and an effective set of links are necessary to make the marketing/NPD integration work. That is, they are necessary in order for your NPD process to fulfill its potential—and to capitalize on the huge opportunity inherent in the current dismal NPD success rate.

Phase 0—Concept Evaluation
Market opportunity
Strategic fit
Operational fit (e.g., sales channels)
Position w. r. t. competition and w. r. t. other company products
Competition identified and SWOT analysis performed
Attractiveness with regard to other opportunities
Examples of specific target customers
Compelling reasons for customer to buy
Competitive advantage or strategic necessity specified
Competitive response
Market and strategic weakness identified and considered
All product dimensions visible to the customer
Reasons *not* to proceed
Marketing resources needed to proceed

Phase 1 — Planning and Specification
Product definition
Competitive analysis — including competitive reactions
Sales/service issues
Market opportunity drill-down — specific customers, messages, channels
Strategic fit and linkages detail
Fit/overlap with existing products defined and resolved
Marketing objectives and success measures defined
Results of concept testing with target customers integrated
Marketing strategy sketched out
Preliminary marketing/promotion plan
Marketing resources necessary delineated and confirmed available from each source
Cross-business unit issues defined and resolved
Resources needed

Figure 12-3

PRODUCT MANAGEMENT AND PRODUCT MARKETING: A MIXED CONCEPT

In most companies, the implementation mechanism for integrating marketing with NPD is in product management and product marketing. Increasingly, in companies today, the Product Manager is the focal point for a product's success. Indeed, the product management concept has been applied throughout all industries — goods and services; B2B and B2C; semi-custom and mass-market.

Surprisingly, there is little commonality from company-to-company regarding just what product management actually is. In some companies, the product manager is the business segment profit-and-loss manager, while, in others, he/she is "simply" the product champion. In some companies, the product manager is responsible primarily for new products—from ideation to product introduction, while, in others, the responsibility centers around maximizing sales of existing products. In some companies, the product manager has full direct-line authority for actions, while, in others, he/she must exert dotted-line influence.

It's no wonder that the body of knowledge regarding product management is so sparse ... and often contradictory!

PRODUCT MANAGEMENT VS. PRODUCT MARKETING

We believe that, again, much of this confusion can be cleared up by viewing the business of a company as a manufacturing facility in which the object is to manufacture customers. Just as in product manufacturing, the product must be designed before it can be produced; in Customer Manufacturing, a product must first be correctly specified to match a market need before it can be successfully sold.

In product manufacturing, design is the responsibility of the engineering department, while production is the province of the manufacturing plant. In Customer Manufacturing, the selection and specification of a new product (or service) is the responsibility of marketing, while sales of the product are the province of the sales force. And, just as there is a phase-over "gray area" in product manufacturing called "manufacturing engineering," so there is a similar crossover area along the marketing-sales continuum called "promotion." (Unfortunately, as discussed earlier, many people confuse promotion with marketing, believing promotion to be all there is to marketing or, at least, all that matters.)

We believe it to be most useful to assign the term "product management" to those activities on the "marketing" side of the continuum and use the term "product marketing" in relation to promotion, sales support, and field marketing — all activities on the promotion and sales side of the marketing-sales continuum. (See Figure 12-4.)

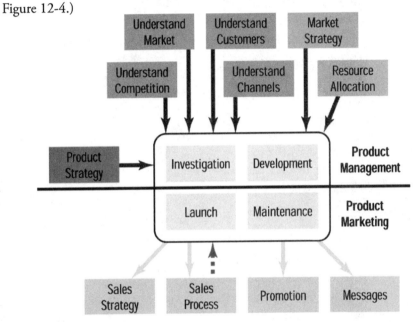

Figure 12-4

•• The Lead User Method

Competitive companies today have had a structured phase-review type product development process in place for some time. A similarly structured marketing process like the Customer Manufacturing System provides the appropriate marketing input — both in content and in depth — at the right time in the NPD process. Most of this information required during the NPD process from marketing is not conceptually difficult to obtain — it's driving a

Another way to make this distinction is to view product management as concerned mostly with new products, while product marketing is concerned primarily with existing products—a gray crossover area around product introduction. We believe that this distinction makes sense, since it aligns these two marketing responsibilities around the skills that people tend to have, the corporate organizations with which they work primarily, and the basis on which they are measured. (See Figure 12-5.) A "product manager" who has true business unit or product-line profit and loss responsibility, and a solid line organi-

155

zation, is really an SBU (Strategic Business Unit) manager.

What this means for increasing the effectiveness of your NPD process, through a better and more complete marketing process, is that you must assign the correct point marketing person to that NPD process. For example, an NPD process concerned with really new products is probably best off with someone from a product-management background. An NPD process concerned with tweaking a product or customizing it for a particular segment may be better off with a product-marketing person.

Perhaps the greatest mistake we've seen over the years is the assignment of a marketing person who, by temperament, skills,

process that consistently delivers it that is the problem that a Customer Manufacturing System solves.

As a result, the really interesting, conceptually difficult, new work in the integration of marketing with product development is at the so-called "fuzzy front end" of product development, usually centering on the "ideation" process. That is, on the spawning of viable new product ideas — not merely line extensions or incremental improve-ments, valuable and necessary as these are — but discovery of whole new products or the opening up of whole new markets.

and organizational "home," is a product-marketing person to a role in the NPD process that should be assigned to a product-management person. This mistake leads not only to failure of the project, but to distrust on the part of NPD professionals of the marketing function overall.

	Product Management	Product Marketing
Time Frame	Ideation to Introduction	Introduction to End of Life
Primary Focus	Product Development	Sales
Skills	Research, Technical, Project Management, Strategic	Promotional, Sales
Measured	On Time, Meets Market Need	Sales, Profits

Figure 12-5

Several techniques have been developed in this space recently, with considerable success. The Lead User method is one such technique, and it's been applied with success repeatedly at 3M. The Lead User method involves the ferreting out of actual users who are themselves pushing the edge of product use, who have application needs well ahead of the market, and who may well have done some limited development or jerry-rigging or prototyping work themselves in order to satisfy their own needs, and then intensively working with them to understand those needs and their drivers.

The existence of such lead users — and their usual willingness to talk to you — is a counter-argument to the oft-heard, but false maxim that it's useless to ask users what they need or want in technology markets since they can't imagine what non-existing technology or products could do for them.

A robustly constructed CMS, particularly the Environmental Influences part of it, demands that you gather information about lead users, and it demands that you gather the information that provides the context for informed decision-making based on your lead user data.

Put a similar way, the Lead User method is one technique of obtaining information that a CMS demands. A CMS, however, does not regard Lead User information as an island, but rather as part of an integrated data set from which all marketing and sales decisions can be made, from specifying market and product direction, to resource allocation, all the way to sales messages.

Making constructive use of Lead User insights is part of the now well-known "innovators dilemma" which faces most companies. An over-arching, full-featured, complete, linked marketing/sales process is a mechanism that forces a rigorous analysis of a company's NPD resource allocation. ● ●

13

CHAPTER THIRTEEN

where are you on your value acceleration journey?

M anagement of successful enterprises in the 21st Century will be vastly different than at any previous time. Gone will be the "can't fail" stable economy and steadily growing markets of the post-WWII era. The time when a company can succeed with sloppy internal processes in spite of itself will be over. Except for the most entrenched players, companies will no longer be able to get away with "testing the waters," learning their lessons, and coming back to succeed another day. Instead, the prevailing rule for 21st Century enterprises will be: "One strike and you're out."

PROCESS — AGAIN

This book has been about both the necessity of process management and about the need for a process model of the corporation's single most critical, non-outsourceable function: marketing/sales. The word "process" has the unfortunate distinction of having been once catapulted into fad status. And — like another perfectly good word and perfectly useable concept, "synergy" — it has since fallen into disrepute. To anyone who has suffered through one of the legion of "re-engineering" failures of the last decade, the word "process" must have a bitter taste, indeed.

Yet to the hundreds of thousands of people who now work in process-driven enterprises—and yes, even re-engineered ones—the word "process" is not unwelcome. In fact, process thinking and management are now so much the part and parcel of enterprise that they permeate everything that's done in well-managed companies.

In the information economy, processes will *be* the company. It is management's job to define those functional and cross-functional processes that will be critical to their success and start to build them now. Two of the functional processes that will be foundational and critical for any business will be their product development process and their marketing/sales process. Companies that have not already instituted high-performance product development processes are already considerably behind the curve. And those companies that have begun to institute a structured marketing/sales process will lead their industries in the next era.

In fact, the acceptance of the necessity of process has been a growing conversation in management circles over the last 10 years. Open any reputable business journal these days and you will find a renewed focus on the fundamentals of business management in the information economy. You will find thoughtful analyses of core process identification and management, with examples from leading companies.

From this viewpoint, it can be argued that the problem with re-engineering is that it didn't go far enough. In the punch-drunk glory days of the re-engineering fad, re-engineering consultants would move into a company, turn everything upside down and rebuild it from scratch. It was like shooting fish in a barrel — and mighty profitable, too! But, all to often, destroying a few dysfunctional bureaucratic walls and designing a new process to handle some necessary activities simply didn't address the real issues.

The facts are there. Look at the companies that have succeeded for more than a few years. Look at the great companies. Examine their management and you will find effective processes at their core. If these companies exist in turbulent markets, you will also find that these processes not only accept change as a necessity, they seek it out and embrace it — change and adaptability are built into the *core process* of these companies.[56]

---

56. As any engineer knows, a system can be designed to be changeable and adaptive, or static — and be nonetheless stable either way.

Many authorities have spoken cogently on this subject, but Clayton Christensen and Michael Overdof describe the situation particularly well, when they write that "One could put two sets of identically capable people to work in different organizations, and what they accomplished would be significantly different. That's because organizations themselves — independent of the people and other resources in them — have capabilities."[57] Christensen and Overdof then go on to explain that a company's processes are one of the three legs of its capabilities.

Over time, as the visionary entrepreneurs leave a company, "the locus of the organization's capabilities shifts toward its process and values… In fact, one reason that so many soaring young companies flame out … [is that] they fail to develop processes that can [sustain them]."[58]

MARKETING/SALES — THE SINE QUA NON

Peter Drucker was right — as he usually is and was for decades — *Marketing is the company and all else are costs.*

We use this definition of marketing: *that faculty which aligns the capabilities of the firm with the desires of the market-place.* What Drucker meant in the first phrase of his famous quote was that "marketing" is what the firm does at its core. What he meant by the second was that everything else can be outsourced: operations, finance, IT, HR, and so on. But figuring out what it is that customers want that you can best provide and managing the firm toward that end is the irreducible function of the firm. That's marketing — and it is the one thing that can't be outsourced.

To this end, managers can begin by evaluating the state of marketing in their company. They should perform a marketing self-examination by asking the following kinds of questions:

- Does our marketing/sales consist of a marketing/sales process or individual marketing/sales activities?

- If we have a marketing/sales process, is it understood? Is it followed? Is it complete? Is it resourced?

57. Meeting the Challenge of Disruptive Change, (Harvard Business Review, March-April, 2000), 68.

58. Ibid, 71.

- How well integrated is any marketing/sales process that we have?

- How well does our marketing/sales process reflect the needs, wants and demands of the market we choose to serve?

- How well do tactical marketing/sales activities flow from marketing strategy?

- How repeatable and stable are our marketing/sales processes?

- How well integrated are our marketing/sales and product development processes?

- How well integrated is marketing/sales planning with corporate strategic planning?

- What structural causes of our last obvious marketing/sales failure are still in place?

- Is our selling process a mirror of our customer's buying process?
  How do we measure and manage the sales process (as opposed to just sales results)?

- Do we feed back the results of our sales process to marketing?

Once a general appreciation for the marketing/sales state of affairs is accomplished through this self-examination, managers should perform a formal marketing/sales audit. The actual marketing/sales process, its tasks, information flows, decision points, and interaction with other groups, should be recorded and plotted onto an "as is" chart. This chart will reveal which existing skills, tasks and process "raw material" the company has to work with. It will also reveal the non-existent, irrelevant, or sub-standard skills, tasks and processes in the company. Next:

- A "should be" process diagram is then generated. Existing resources should be deployed to this new process, and the work of fully realizing it is then begun.

- (It is critical to note that the "should be" process is not a modified version of the existing process. It is truly the "should be" process. In other words, the process you need to accomplish the results desired. While this new process may be a modification of your existing process, it is important that you not start with that end in mind, but rather, with a clean sheet of paper to develop the right process for your needs. Moving from the "as is" process to the new, "should be" process is what happens next.)

- The main constraint to performance and/or achieving the "should be" state should be identified — along with the appropriate time-frame assumption and other assumptions made in identifying that constraint. Work should begin immediately on eliminating this constraint.

- Areas for elimination of waste are identified and elimination efforts undertaken right away.

- Appropriate process measurement points are established and continuous improvement instituted throughout every measurable step in the process

Moving from the "as is" state to the "should be" state of marketing/sales process will undoubtedly involve much talent and hard work along all of management's many dimensions. It will involve designing a new marketing organization and, possibly, a new sales organization as well, around existing pieces, putting some new elements in place, instituting periodic state reviews, and forging tight links with the product development process.

We advise companies wanting to initiate a unified marketing/sales process to start with a pilot program, composed of willing volunteers, and independent enough to succeed with its own resources. Nothing succeeds like success. Once this group or project demonstrates the potential of the new way of doing things, other groups will tend to jump on the bandwagon.

FINAL WORDS

St. Augustine said, "The higher your structure is to be, the deeper must be its foundation." This is certainly true of the corporation in the 21st Century. As markets change frenetically, as massive amounts of capital rush to fund the best new ideas and as the cost of missing the market increases, a company's process foundation must be very strong and deep, indeed.

Yet, we have arrived at a conflict in professional management. On the one hand, it is now widely recognized that process orientation and process management is the essence of effective performance. On the other hand, we have managed to effectively process-manage every function in the firm except the one that ultimately matters most: marketing/sales. The reason that this irreducible function remains a bastion of seat-of-the-pants management, even in well-managed companies, is that there hasn't been a good process model with which to manage it. There hasn't existed a practical mental representation of the organization of the function—in detail, with linkages in place—so that a competent manager could know whether the process was working, could measure it and could improve it effectively.

Within a few years, the primary business of any company may be different in almost all respects from the one it's in now. The only way to survive in this kind of environment is to establish a deep foundation of corporate processes that work continuously and synchronously to anticipate the new market, to identify the alignment between these processes and the enterprise's capabilities, and to guide the organization in adapting.

The companies leading the charge in the information economy have instituted a structured product development process now. But, without a coherent marketing/sales process, even the world's best product development process is doomed to irrelevance.

The last 50 years have not only demonstrated the effectiveness of process management beyond all doubt, they have given us a rich set of proven process management tools. These insights have been major drivers of increased enterprise value. They have generated an explosion in the value delivered by the enterprise to customers, and as a result, the value of the enterprise itself has grown. This constant increase in value — the value "velocity" of the enterprise, if you will — will not cease. Woe be to the management that does not constantly increase the value of its company to its customers. The focus in well-managed companies is thus on increasing its value velocity — or on value acceleration. And the place to focus that effort has now migrated to the marketing/sales process. By using an appropriate process model of marketing/sales, management has the ability to apply verified process management tools to marketing/sales, and this will close the last remaining gap in the process management of the enterprise.

An effective marketing/sales process is the *sine qua non* of the enterprise's existence.

Index

References to footnotes (n), boxes (b), and figures (f) are indicated by an italicized letter following the page number.

MITCHELL E. GOOZÉ

Mitch Goozé is the president and founder of the Customer Manufacturing Group. His broad scope of business experience ranges from operations management in established firms, to start-up and turn-around situations and mergers. A seasoned general manager, he has headed divisions of large corporations and been CEO of independent firms, always focusing the company strategy on the most important person in business — the customer. Prior to founding Customer Manufacturing Group, Mitch was president of Teledyne Components, a division of Teledyne, Inc., from 1985 through 1990.

Mitch's unique expertise in determining strategic positioning at the corporate or product level has resulted in the cornerstone element of the Customer Manufacturing System— Value Specification. For years he has used his *Who, What and How* assessment methods to help companies define what their customers are buying that they can't get from anyone else. As a recognized expert in marketing, strategic business planning, and customer relationships, Mitch has been invited to speak to business groups across the globe. His ideas have helped thousands of senior executives to gain a competitive advantage in their market through the assessment and redesign of their System to Manufacture Customers.

Mitch is a past member of the Board of Directors of The American Electronics Association and ASUCLA, and The Board of Advisors of the Leavy School of Business at Santa Clara University. He is a founder of the International Center for Professional Speaking in Phoenix, AZ.

Mitch has been an invited guest speaker and published author for over twenty years. *The Secret To Selling More: It's Not Where You've Been Looking, If It Were, You'd Have Found It Already* (IMI 2001, 2005) is his second book focused on sales and marketing. His first book *It's Not Rocket Science: Using Marketing to Build A Sustainable Business* (IMI 1997, 2002) was released in trade paperback in 2002.

Mitch is a graduate of the University of California, Los Angeles (UCLA). He did graduate work in electrical engineering at the California State University, Long Beach, and graduate business studies at Santa Clara University. He received his MBA from the Edinburgh Business School, Heriot-Watt University, Edinburgh, Scotland.

Mitchell Goozé can be reached via e-mail at mgooze@customermfg.com or by phone at 408.496.4585.

RALPH MROZ

Since 1978, Ralph Mroz has managed or implemented nearly every step of the marketing process. His experience spans hands-on tactics to corporate strategic planning, encompassing large corporations, small companies, as well as start-ups.

Ralph brings years of experience in the research and analytical aspects of marketing. He helps clients to fully integrate marketing and product development processes, enabling them to successfully enter a new market with a new or an existing product set.

His market-entry expertise has been applied within large corporations such as Hewlett-Packard's power supply division and Digital Equipment Corporation's component and CAD divisions. As one of the original members of Encore Computer Corporation during its start-up, Ralph drafted the market entry plan for an entirely new class of computer. He was also a founder of The Kensington Group, which is the industry standard source for comparative benchmark data on the public relations specialty of Analyst Relations.

Since 1991, he has consulted to companies on competitive positioning and marketing process development. Ralph is a noted proponent of the concept of converting marketing functions to a hierarchical process that is stable, repeatable, and integrates seamlessly with Product Development and Sales. His article, "The Synchronous Marketing Process" (May, 1998, *Industrial Marketing Management*), is the first to describe in detail an over-arching, consistent and measurable marketing process. This concept is a key element of the Customer Manufacturing System.

Ralph holds a B.S. in Electrical Engineering and an M.B.A. from the University of Massachusetts at Amherst.

Ralph Mroz can be reached via e-mail at rmroz@customermfg.com or by phone at 413.774.3512.